THE BUDDHA

The Story
of an
Awakened Life

DAVID KHERDIAN

White Cloud Press
Ashland, Oregon

Inquiries should be addressed to:
White Cloud Press, PO Box 3400, Ashland, Oregon 97520.
Website: www.whitecloudpress.com

First printing: 2004

Cover design by David Ruppe, Impact Publications
"The Bodhisattva Padmapani, Ajanta, India" © Graham Harrison
Interior design by Christy Collins

Printed in the United States of America

Library of Congress Cataloging-in-Publication Data

Library of Congress Cataloging-in-Publication Data
Kherdian, David.
The Buddha : the story of an awakened life / by David Kherdian.
p. cm.
ISBN 1-883991-63-3 (pbk.)
1. Gautama Buddha. 2. Buddhists--India--Biography. 3.
Buddhism--Doctrines. I. Title.
BQ882.K48 2004
294.3'63--dc22

2003025142

A Selection of Other Books
by David Kherdian

On a Spaceship with Beelzebub: By a Grandson of Gurdjieff

Monkey: A Journey to the West

The Road From Home

Seeds of Light: Poems from a Gurdjieff Community

The Revelations of Alvin Tolliver

The Song in the Walnut Grove

Letters to My Father (Fall, 2004)

one

OUR BUDDHA WAS born in the foothills of the Himalayas, where the fertile fields of the Ganges Valley rise gradually into hills and purple mountains, whose peaks carry the eternal snows of myth and legend.

His father, King Suddhodana, was the ruler of the Shakya state, a small country whose capital city was Kapilavastu. King Suddhodana belonged to the clan lineage of the Gautamas. His wife, Mahamaya, was the daughter of a powerful Shakyan noble. She was better known as Maya, which meant illusion, a name that fitted her perfectly, for it was said of her that she was as beautiful as a girl in a dream. She was of noble character, pious and wise, and abhorred the sins of the flesh, immodest behavior, cruelty and unkindness. Her only regret in life was being childless. She yearned and prayed that a son would be given unto her. Much of her time was spent visiting temples where she prayed and made offerings.

Her husband was patient, reminding her of the prophesy of a wandering Rishi. "Have you forgotten the look on his face," he said to his wife, "when, gazing up at our palace, he declared, 'Here a child shall be born, who will be a ruler among men, truly a king of kings.'"

Looking back at her husband, Maya smiled, afraid to speak because tears had already begun to well up in her eyes.

"We will attend the Festival of the Full Moon of Midsummer, which begins on the morrow," the king declared. The next day, dressed in royal robes, they mounted their prize elephant and led the parade through the town. They were followed by sacred cows that had garlands of flowers strewn over their horns. The men sang in chorus while horns blew and confetti rained on the adoring crowd, while dancing maidens, adorned in spangled skirts and ankle bells, wove among the gathering throng.

The festivities continued for one week. On the final day, Maya arose from her bed, bathed herself in scented water, and went into the city, where she distributed gold pieces to the poor as alms.

She returned to her room, exhausted, and without undressing lay down on her bed and fell instantly into a deep sleep of dreams.

When she awoke, her husband was at her side, rubbing his eyes, having wakened at the same moment. Maya looked longingly at her husband before speaking. "The four kings of Divine Guidance just carried me to the purified waters of a mountain lake where I was bathed in the heavenly waters of paradise, purifying me of every stain. And then, instantly, I was clothed in a flowing gold garment and carried to a veranda atop a silver mountain, where appeared a lordly six-tusked elephant, also silver colored.

"The child shall be born when the Flower-Star shines in the East!" her husband exclaimed.

"Please! Wait!" Maya beseeched him. "Can it be so? Oh yes, the elephant was carrying a pink lotus in its trunk. It was then it trumpeted, racing around me three times before striking me on my right side. And then, with that, it melted into vapor, disappearing in the air. But what is strange is that I did not feel its presence in my side but in my womb, that it had entered in some mysterious way."

They both fell silent and embraced each other, feeling gratitude and joy that was beyond the power of words.

With great pomp and ceremony, the king summoned his Brahmins to court, along with soothsayers, priests, and wise men. After listening intently to Maya's dream-story, the wise men spoke with near unanimity, in separate but linked sentences, acknowledging the presence of a miracle that was clear, equally, to each of them. "This beginning can have but two endings," said one.

"But not necessarily," said the next.

"There will be great joy, for he will be a fitting descendant."

"And worthy."

The king interjected. "Why two endings?"

"If he chooses a worldly life and remains in the palace he will become a universal monarch, the greatest we've seen."

"But if he renounces his position of power and wealth he will become a wanderer, a holy man, and one day a completely enlightened buddha . . ."

"Who will provide the world with the elixir of deathlessness."

"Yes, for his response to suffering will be the deciding factor."

The king was pleased and gave out rich gifts to his Brahmins and arranged a feast for all his people.

Maya returned to her chambers in great joy and wonder. Invisible gods moved at her side and she was never again alone. In the days ahead, she had but to rest and ponder her fate and that of her son. The months passed for her in quietude and serenity.

When the time of her son's arrival grew near, she said to Suddhodana, "It is time for me to return to my parental home in Devadaha, as is the custom with the women of my family."

The king of course agreed and made great preparations for her departure.

For the long day's journey, Maya was outfitted with a palanquin, along with servants and courtiers. When they had journeyed as far as Lumbini Garden, they paused for a rest. Maya descended from her carriage and began to walk inside the park. The spring flowers were in bloom and birds were calling from the trees. She stopped to listen to the cry of a distant peacock while standing in the green shade of an ashoka tree. When she looked up, the overhanging branches swooned over her, protectively, and in that instant she gave birth to her son. He appeared before her in a transparent sphere of liquid light as a completed being, but in miniature, and then in the next instant he was wrapped in a saffron robe at her breast and she was cooing in his ear, the sweet perfume of her breath on his forehead.

It was evening when they arrived at the palace gate, their pathway lit by something more than the moon's fullness, for the light of heaven shone with such brilliance that even the dark, shadowy earth was lit, as if night were day and the moon an evening sun.

In a remote cave, deep in the Himalayas, a renowned rishi penetrated the mystery of the holy birth, and guided by the light that shone from above, was directed to the gate of the king.

The holy man, by name Asita, was ushered into the great hall to be met by his lord, who was himself deeply honored by the rishi's visit. But it was the rishi who had come to make obeisance. "I have traveled here to witness the arrival of the holy one," he said. The king was pleased and commanded the prince to be brought into the room.

Asita gazed upon the golden countenance of the holy prince, and bowing, placed the child's feet upon his forehead. "I see now with plain sight what I knew I would find here. The thirty-two major and eighty minor marks of a great being are present on his body. For such a one there can be but two destinies, that of a universal monarch, or of an enlightened buddha," he said, hesitating and turning his face from the king before continuing, "who will live a life of homelessness while traveling the spiritual path."

"Two possibilities?" the king questioned aloud, before sinking into his chair. "These were the words of my Brahmins, but I did not hear the first time these words were spoken what this could mean. I could lose my son to the world. And if this were to happen, what then will the world mean to me?"

The king's reverie was interrupted suddenly by the rishi's sobs.

"But why do you cry?" the king asked, thinking not of the rishi but of himself.

5

"I cry in happiness for the glory that this birth portends, and I cry in sorrow that I will not be here to see it unfold."

"But you are an enlightened being!" The king exclaimed.

"I have not yet attained to the ultimate realization," Asita sighed. "The world will soon be bathed in a great light, but I will not be here to see its radiance, or to receive its gifts."

two

THE RISHI MUMBLED something under his breath as he was escorted from the palace that was heard only by one of the king's attendants. "The queen mother will pass away in seven days. The king will be sorely tested. Already the preparations have begun for her grand reception as the Motherhead of the coming Buddha. The king's sorrow will now equal his glory. Poor king! Poor king! For every gain there must be a loss, from every loss a great gain!"

The prophetic words of the rishi soon became the king's experience. For the seven days that Maya lived, a dark cloud shadowed the palace walls, as if to prepare its inhabitants, who would have to bring into balance the immeasurable gain of a divinely born prince with the death of their treasured queen.

The king was bereft. With the loss of his wife, his radiant happiness brought about by his son's birth was now shattered. He could not eat or sleep, his mind torn in two by the violent collision of his great gain, followed almost immediately by the unbearable loss of his beloved wife.

He had named his son Siddhartha, "He who has attained." But with that he seemed to break his filial connection, retreating into silence in order to nurture his grief in private.

Maya's sister, Mahapajapati, took upon herself the role of living mother to the baby prince.

Time passed, and when the king's period of mourning had been completed, and his sanity restored, he and Mahapajapati married.

Siddhartha's new mother loved the child as her own, and carefully arranged his days. The prince would have thirty-two nurses, eight to carry him, eight to give him milk, eight to bathe him, and eight to play with him. To see that his senses were enriched, the king created three lotus-pools, separately flowered with blue, white, and red lotus-flowers. Siddhartha's clothes and colognes came from Benares, and when he was old enough to walk he was given a white umbrella to shade him and protect him from the harmful elements.

The auspicious birth of the coming buddha had settled over the land, gladdening even the animals, while the people moved through their days with a loving regard for one another, and with humility and grace. This grace was a foretelling, a shadow of the future cast over the present as a promise and as a gift that would, in time, need to be earned.

Siddhartha was raised with his cousins, Ananda and Devadatta.

Ananda would become his closest friend and ally. They were taught sporting and warrior skills, such as archery, wrestling, and horsemanship, as well as chariot-racing. Although Siddhartha excelled at all these martial arts, it wasn't long before he turned away from athletic sports. Competition did not particularly interest him. He would at times deliberately miss the target when shooting with his bow, so as not to hurt his opponent's feelings.

He was particularly repelled by hunting. Instead of going to the fields and woods with his cousins, he would wander off by himself to be alone with his thoughts.

He was also an outstanding student, excelling in math and music. By eight years old, he was already proficient in all the alphabets of India and he could even read the puzzling ideographs of the Mongols and Chinese. He took up the flute, and the haunting melodies he played in his chambers would waft through the corridors, bringing tears of joy to Mahapajapati's heart.

From an early age, Siddhartha was drawn to nature. He would often be found sitting cross-legged under a banyan tree in deep contemplation. One day, he felt a deer approach the open ground near where he sat. It raised its head, returning Siddhartha's stare, and seemed not to be startled when the prince began to speak. "You know why you are here," he said to the deer, "to eat, sleep, fight and procreate, and all of this without a single doubt or forethought. But why am I here? So much has been made possible for me, there are so many choices, but where in all this can I find the meaning that will reveal the truth of my life?"

In the next instant, he was distracted by the call of wild swans

flying overhead. One of the birds veered out of line and crashed at
his feet, an arrow lodged in its wing. Startled, Siddhartha jumped
to his feet and seized the bird, gently raising it from the ground.
While speaking to it in a low voice, he removed the arrow with great
care and staunched the wound with wild honey.

Devadatta came racing out of the woods, waving his bow. "Give
me that bird; I killed it and it is mine."

"You did not kill it, you only stopped its flight." Siddhartha
said, holding the bird close to his breast.

Ananda interceded. "Stop this arguing," he declared, "and take
the swan home to show your father and let him decide."

Devadatta and Siddhartha begrudgingly agreed, jostling as they
walked towards the palace gates. They often argued and fought.
Devadatta was aggressive and haughty, and seemed to know what
he wanted, while Siddhartha was often moody and withdrawn.
Devadatta took this as criticism, and perhaps secretly it was, because
they clashed over principles, about which they had yet no name, but
with feelings that were strong and already unchangeable, and would
in time reveal the meaning and destiny of their different characters.

The king summoned his Brahmins. After a short conference,
they stated that the bird belonged to Siddhartha by right of mercy.
"For he who saves life," they proclaimed, "has dominion over the
slayer of life."

In his sixteenth year Siddhartha attended the spring plowing festival for the first time. Although quiet and thoughtful, he was caught
up with the others in the gaiety and splendor of the occasion,

watching the oxen that were brightly caparisoned, pulling brightly painted plows, while children ran excitedly about, and the musicians played music appropriate for the occasion. Siddhartha was touched by everyone's happiness, but as the day wore on, he became aware that in preparing the soil for planting, a great disruption was taking place in the animal world. Bird's nests were being plowed under and snakes were cut in two, while rabbits and ground squirrels were seen running from their burrowed homes. The monkeys fled through the trees, screaming and gesticulating at the humans. But they were hardly noticed by the invading throng that seemed to be aware only of themselves. Siddhartha was greatly disturbed because he could feel the suffering, not only of the animals, but of the earth itself.

Siddhartha quietly withdrew to a rose apple tree, where he sat in deep concentration. "Is it right for life to bring death and for death to give life," he pondered. He closed his eyes, hoping in silence to find the answer in himself, wishing desperately to be reconciled from this hideous paradox.

He began by asking himself if man could live without causing suffering to himself and to others. "Above all," he asked the heavens, "how is man to conquer his own suffering? Clearly, since it cannot be eliminated, something else is required. Is that not so?"

The earth revolved slowly away from the sun while Siddhartha sat in utter repose, aware only of the dilemma that consumed him. Late in the afternoon, his father appeared at his side and gazed in silence at his son's trance-like state, realizing that something profoundly important was taking place. It was then he noticed that the shadow cast from the rose apple tree had remained motionless during all the long hours of his son's meditation, protecting him from the shifting rays of the sun.

The king became worried and held council with his Brahmins. "I fear the Prince has turned melancholic. Yesterday I found him in a trance-like state, sitting under the protective shade of a rose apple tree. I fear the worst, that the fates are conspiring to take him from me into an ascetic life of self-denial."

The Brahmins listened carefully before speaking. "He will not be easily diverted," said one.

Another argued, "He is surrounded by sensual delights—provocative maidens, scented gardens, sumptuous foods. . ."

"Nothing is lacking," the king shouted. "I have seen to that."

"This prince cannot be bound by chains of pleasure, but only lightly with a woman's hair."

"They are here in abundance, for his pleasure and satisfaction," the king retorted.

"Not all, not any—but one! The joy of true love exceeds that of mere pleasure, which is fleeting and easily sated. But what touches the heart remains in the heart and grows and matures, like aging wine."

The king was pleased, feeling they had delivered him from his dilemma. "It is time for the Prince to marry, then!" he exclaimed, "but to whom?"

The Brahmins nodded. "For some time, we have kept our watch over the beautiful princess Yasodhara, who lives but a short distance from here. We will arrange a contest in which Siddhartha will challenge all comers for the winning prize that will then be awarded by the young maiden. If Siddhartha triumphs, and we are confident he will, they will meet in a manner most compelling—for women wish to be won, but only by the fittest, for a woman's heart is a secret chamber that only love can unlock."

Siddhartha was aware that the prize for the victor would be awarded by the acclaimed Yasodhara, who was known to him only by name. He approached the contest with a light heart, knowing he would enjoy the event no matter the outcome, for a new freedom and expansiveness had come over him since his experience under the rose apple tree.

Yasodhara was known far and wide, not only for her great beauty but for her gentleness and humility, and not least of all for her devotion to her father. Siddhartha had listened to the stories about her while observing her from a distance. He was struck not only by her grace and beauty, but by her shyness, that told him she was someone like himself, who cared more for privacy than attention. Something in this gave her an aura of mystery and aloofness that made him want to know her.

The young men were too proud to speak of their feelings about her to one another, but it was clear from their posture and bearing as they met on the plain that this was not an ordinary contest; something in their young manhood was being tested and judged.

Siddhartha met his rivals on his father's turf, for they were the challengers and he the resplendent prince, and the one they had come to conquer in order to win the prize from the maiden's hand.

Mounted on his steed, Kantaka, Siddhartha met his challengers on the playing field.

Devadatta was the easy victor at wrestling, and although Siddhartha had come out on top in all the other events—horse racing, sword play, and the racing of the steeds, it was the final race of the chariots that carried the most points and could result in a tie between Devadatta and Siddhartha, if Siddhartha were to finish last.

It was the inherent violence in chariot racing that made it a crowd favorite, and with the contention that existed between Devadatta and Siddhartha, this was the race the crowd anxiously awaited.

But the contest was over almost as it began, with Siddhartha's chariot seeming to rise above the playing field, sweeping by Devadatta and Ananda with such fury, swiftness, and certainty that not a whiff of dust was raised—as would have been expected—and with Siddhartha leaving his opponents behind as mere witnesses to his glorious victory.

When it was done, they stood in a straight line before the raised platform from where Yasodhara descended to present the prizes. Each contestant would receive something. As they gracefully received their prize, Devadatta and Ananda took a step backward, until at last Siddhartha stood alone. He now stepped forward to meet the Princess Yasodhara. As the ultimate winner, he was given the laurel wreath. As she placed the crown upon his head, their eyes met for the first time. What they felt for each other at that moment could not be concealed; there was an instant recognition, older than time, for they knew at that moment that an eternal bond had been made that could never be broken.

From that day on, Yasodhara and Siddhartha were continually together. In the evenings they dined with the King and Queen Mother, but their days were spent alone, wandering the palatial grounds, bathing themselves in the surrounding beauty of nature that seemed to reflect their feelings for one another. Siddhartha carefully guided her to his favorite haunts, taking her at last to the rose apple tree, where they embraced for the first time and where he proposed to her and received her blushing assent.

He then told her of the vision he had received of life's potential need and possibility for universal harmony, and although she did not have the words or experience to express what she felt, she knew intuitively, as he had, that it was in this inward turning that he had been shown his destiny. And she, as his helpmate, was convinced she had found her place in his life.

three

THE WEDDING OF Prince Siddhartha and Yasodhara was celebrated throughout the kingdom. Lanterns and banners were hung from the eaves of homes and buildings, and flowers were placed in every nook and crannie. Music chimed through the streets in competing melodies that somehow merged and blended. It was a great time for storytellers, dancing girls, and jugglers—for all shared and expressed in their own way the joy that love brings to all who reside in its presence.

Inside the palace walls mantras were sung and gifts bestowed upon the king's Brahmins. Alms and temple offerings were also made. And blessings, joyous and everlasting.

The garments of the bride and bridegroom were tied in age-old ceremony, with seven steps to be taken three times around the fire, after which two straws were set adrift upon the reddened milk, to prove that love exists until parted by death.

King Suddhodana was deeply pleased and whispered his confidence to the Brahmin closest to him in attendance. The Brahmin answered, "The triad is not yet finished, for the binding to be complete there must be duty to the realm, his wife, and then a child."

The king demurred. "Will we be safe then?"

The Brahmin answered only with an enigmatic smile, leaving the king to ponder his own doubts and misgivings.

King Suddhodana decided he would ensnare his son with sensual pleasures. Three palaces were built for the prince and his bride, one for winter, another for summer, and a third for the rainy season. Each was built from different materials: marble, polished wood, and stone, and each uniquely placed: in winter to attract the sun, in summer for shade, and in the rainy season among low-growing trees of fan-shaped leaves. And everywhere there were pools with jewel-colored fish, tamarind and asoka trees, parrots and cooing doves, as well as monkeys and gentle gazelles, for the king understood Siddhartha's belief that nothing was closer to God than animals and little children.

To insure his happiness and to be certain he would not have time for any distracting thoughts, the king provided musicians, storytellers and jugglers, and most importantly, dancing girls, who were the fairest and most beautiful that could be found, their beauty meant to intoxicate and subdue Siddhartha, should he grow weary of his bride.

And yet, with all his preparations, the king remained doubtful, complaining to his wife, Mahapajapati. "How am I to cage my son, this bird of Heaven, whose greatest fault is compassion, who cares only for the sufferings of others. This is what his eyes tell me, and his glance, but what is in his mind, this I cannot penetrate.

"And yet, if I can eliminate the experience of suffering, he might forget what it is he must remember. Therefore, old age, illness, and death must be removed from his sight, that he might learn to conquer without conscience, and not succumb to the sympathies of the heart."

"You cannot make him what he is not."

"You heard the ministers, he is pinioned between the twin pillars of the lord and the lowly monk."

"Why lowly? Is it lowly to serve?"

"Who cannot be a monk. But to be a king. . . ."

The queen fell silent and soon left the room, knowing that the argument, as always, was being waged inside her husband's head, but also that the outcome was outside his mortal power. For she knew that Siddhartha's struggle was with his own soul, and that the outcome was outside of her husband's or anyone else's influence.

The palaces were built inside the walls of the kingdom, whose gates, tightly guarded, were constructed of iron mounts that made a loud, clamorous noise whenever opened, so that the king would know, night and day, if anyone left or entered.

But it was not enough to keep the outside world away, he must detain Siddhartha from seeing that world, or any reminders of that world, which included aging, feebleness, and death. These must be eliminated from his sight at all times.

The lawns and gardens were manicured daily, for even the fading rose had to be plucked and withdrawn from the prince's sight. Falling leaves were swept and burned, and there were no barren branches on any of the trees.

The melancholy prince, who was once content to wander the woods and meadows, and to play his flute over the open waters to the swaying, arching rhythms of the white swans, began to be drawn more and more into the pleasures of the flesh, for all of his senses had slowly been opened to the languid seductions of the body—the eating of the finest foods, including his favorite sherberts cooled by the fresh snows of the Himalayas, lovemaking, and the seductive tones of the sitar and the mandolin.

In this way the years followed one another without any seeming purpose or meaning until, at last, a son was born to Siddhartha and Yasodhara. The king heralded the event as the completion of the triad once revealed by the Brahmins that would, he believed, bind Siddhartha to his princely duties. But instead, it would soon prove to be the undoing of the king's master plan.

With the birth of his son and the deep love that he felt for him, Siddhartha's reasoning capacity, lulled to sleep for so long, began to awaken. In seeing the beginning of life, that he had now produced, he began once again to question the meaning of life's existence and duration.

four

On THE NEXT evening that Siddhartha and Yasodhara dined with the king and queen, Siddhartha announced his intention to journey to Lumbini Park.

"But why?" the king asked. "What can you find there that you don't already have here?"

"Perhaps that is what I am going to find out."

The king fell silent, but the Queen Mother looked at her son and smiled her approval. Turning to her, Siddhartha said, "I want to return to the place of my birth, my mother's favorite park, where you have told me she often went in her youth when she wanted to be alone with her thoughts. I believe there is something waiting for me there."

A proclamation was issued by the king that the roadway leading through the town be prepared for the Prince's passing. The aged, the ill, the lepers, and the crippled would not be allowed in the streets. The citizens were not permitted to remove the dead from their homes or to burn them before nightfall. The homes along the way were canopied in flowing varicolored silks, with tapestries hung from the windows. And with fresh flowers on every sill. Water carriers sprinkled the cobbled streets and incense had been lit along the way.

Siddhartha was accompanied by his closest friend, Ananda, who feared what this trip might reveal to his beloved cousin. Ananda, with the others, had been sworn to secrecy, but he knew in his heart that the king's plan was doomed.

Criers marched ahead with drums and gongs to herald the Prince's passing and to insure that the streets were not defiled in any way.

But hardly had they passed through the Eastern Gate when an aged man, leaning on his cane, stood before the caravan with his withered arm outstretched, asking for alms of the Prince. Siddhartha looked down at the man who remained bowed, not from reverence but from age. His bald, liver-spotted head, reddened blotchy eyes, and withered skin frightened the Prince. "What is this?" he asked, turning to Channa, his charioteer, for an explanation.

"This, my Prince, is old age," answered Channa.

"What is old age then?"

Holding the horses steady, the charioteer answered. "The years advance and bring us to this. This man was once an infant, like your son, and then again he was in the prime of manhood, as you are. But now, my lord, he has come to the end of his days."

"Does this fate then await my father?" Siddhartha asked.

"Yes, my lord, just as it awaits you. But that time is far off. Fear not, my prince, your life is yet ahead of you."

Siddhartha fell silent as the chariot moved ahead, never suspecting that this ghost of a man who had stumbled before him was a Divinity in disguise, seen only by Channa, himself, and his companion Ananda.

He was awakened from his reverie by the cheering in the streets, the smell of incense, and the distracting beauty of flowing silks and waving tapestries. Siddhartha acknowledged the cheering crowd, but his mind was elsewhere.

Once again, time came to a stop for the Prince, for there at the curb was a man, stricken with illness, lying helpless and alone.

"What is this?" Siddhartha asked in a shaking voice.

"This man seems to be stricken with an incurable illness," Channa answered.

"Illness? Incurable? What is that?" the Prince implored.

"It means he can not get well again, but must suffer without hope of recovery."

Once again the prince fell silent. The caravan moved forward past the gathering throng. When they reached the outskirts of town, they were halted by a party crossing the road and bearing a corpse on a litter. Siddhartha was startled by the forlorn sight of this lifeless figure and the wailing bearers tearing at their clothes and covering themselves with ashes.

Shaken to his very core, Siddhartha turned his ashen face to Channa for some explanation. "My lord, this is death. This man is no more. His spirit has vanished. His body has no more life than a lump of coal. He will never again rise and walk. He has left the living for the dead, where all must go in the course of time. This is the end, as it will be for all of us one day."

Siddhartha was shattered, realizing in an instant that the very meaning of life—if there *was* a meaning to life—had been withheld from him. But he of course did not know what his father knew—only what his father had done—for he was not aware of the prophecy made at his birth.

Now at last it had happened. The Prince knew what all his subjects had long known, that life is suffering, and that a man's destiny is controlled by forces outside his power. Channa and Ananda were relieved, for the secret was out and a certain responsibility had been lifted from their shoulders. They would no longer have to conspire in the deluding of the prince.

They had reached the park and were about to enter when Siddhartha, who had been brooding in silence, asked the chariot to stop, that he be allowed to walk the rest of the way. He had no sooner set forth on the path into the park when, seemingly from nowhere, a monk appeared, erect in bearing, with an aura of serenity and detachment about him that was clearly evident to any who could see. As he passed their party, he turned and gazed into Siddhartha's eyes, in a look that made Siddhartha feel that he had been seen, truly seen, for the very first time in his life.

five

SINCE THAT FATEFUL day in the park, Siddhartha had become withdrawn and rarely spoke to anyone. Keeping his own counsel, he came to the fateful decision that he would renounce everything in favor of a monk's life and become homeless, but free.

His son had awakened a long dormant need in Siddhartha to fulfill his destiny. For too long, he had given way to sensual pleasures and the luxury of an easy life. But this new life that he was witnessing in his son reminded him that he must first be responsible to himself.

But what then of his son, and what of his wife, whose being seemed to be inseparable from his own? If he were to leave all this behind, as he knew he must, what would become of them, and what would he become without them? Yet, despite his grief, he knew in his heart that they would be safe and cared for. The greatness he felt inspired to simultaneously brought to him the lowest feelings he had ever had about himself.

Once again, he withdrew into the solitude of nature, where his reason could be purified and his decision, whatever it was to be, would become inviolate.

"The higher the goal, the greater the sacrifice." The words came to him unbidden, and he knew that he had heard the truth, whether or not the words had emanated from him or not. He had achieved, seemingly without his consent or approval, the station of a prince. To renounce this would be the greatest loss possible on the plane of life. But this very sacrifice, if it could be made, would open him to another level, above the plane of ordinary life.

He had come to realize that there was only one real freedom, and that this freedom could not be achieved in confinement, or by the privileges of caste.

Siddhartha called Ananda to his side and confided to his friend all that was in his heart. "I must tell someone of my intention and my plan and I know that I can trust you to keep my secret."

Ananda nodded his assent and followed Siddhartha's gaze toward the heavens, whose jeweled lights seemed to be speaking to the prince.

"When the waxing moon turns full, Ananda, I must depart. You know what I seek and why I must go, and that I may never return, and that if I do it will not be as the one that I am now."

"But how . . ."

"Let me finish, Ananda. I cannot tell Yasodhara or my parents.

The king would not understand and I wish most of all to spare them any additional suffering. By not knowing, they can believe what they like, each according to their understanding of who I am and what I am called to do. It is not as if they did not know that this day might one day come."

"You have placed a great burden upon me if I am not to speak."

"Your loss of me is as my loss of you. This we can endure, although apart. But I can tell you this, we will meet again."

"But not Yasodhara, the king . . ."

"Yasodhara will understand, but only if she comes to it by herself. This will take time.

"Let us say no more. The moon brightens as we speak, tomorrow or the next day I will be gone. But as the moon diminishes and then returns, I too will one day reappear, but where, for whose sake, and for how long, neither the moon nor I can say."

On the following evening, Siddhartha knew that the time for his departure had arrived. He waited until midnight when all were asleep before calling Channa and telling him to bring his mount, Kantaka. When Kantaka approached his master, Siddhartha was struck by his white coat that seemed to be a reflection of the moon's light in guiding him safely on the path—the moon to show the way, his white steed to take him safely there.

With Channa holding the bridle, they moved soundlessly through the open courtyard. The immense gate was opened without sound by the guiding Divinities that had come to play their part. They quickly passed the sleeping guards and entered the waiting forest, where Siddhartha dismounted and revealed his intentions to

Channa. He removed the jewelry from his wrists and fingers, and the ornaments from his neck. "Take these to my mother and father." After cutting off his topknot and diadem, Siddhartha slowly removed his clothes and changed into a coarse yellow garment that resembled the robe he had seen the monk wearing outside Lumbini Park. "Tell my father that what he tried to prevent me from seeing is what I now go to seek, for I intend to conquer death through deathlessness, that all sentient beings be released from the endless round of senseless suffering that seems to be man's lot."

"How is this possible?" Channa asked, choking back his tears. The Prince was barely recognizable to him now, and he knew that he might never set eyes on his lord again.

"I do not know, Channa, I know only that it must be possible, and that I will devote my life to finding out how."

Channa turned away from the prince with great reluctance and sorrow and began to lead Kantaka away. But Kantaka's heart was broken, and it was evident he would never reach home again. In losing his master, he had lost his will to live. In taking Siddhartha out of the palace grounds and into the wilderness of his new existence, he had completed his mission in life and could now return to his heavenly home.

Siddhartha was about to enter the forest but turned to have one final look at the palace that glowed in the distance. Instead, he was met with the apparition of Mara, the Evil Tempter.

"Get thee away, Mara!" Siddhartha exclaimed. "I know you well who governed over me through my father in the court of sensual delights. You who feed on the illusions of mortal man, leading us astray under the spell of our own weaknesses that you exploit for your own sick glory."

"Do not be deceived, great Prince," Mara answered. "In seven days the golden wheel of empire will turn in your hands, and you shall rule over the four great continents and their attendant islands."

"I have set out," Siddhartha replied with finality. "I will master my destiny and deliver mankind from the grip of your mastery, for I am no longer under your spell."

Seeing that Siddhartha had gone free, Mara dissolved, whispering, "I shall be your invisible shadow, and all your thoughts of lust, cruelty, and malice shall report to me."

Siddhartha laughed pridefully and turned on his way, but in that instant the thought came to him that he had renounced everything, but he had not yet renounced himself.

He had not wandered far into the forest when he came upon a monk foraging in the undergrowth. They greeted each other by pressing their palms together and bowing. The monk asked Siddhartha to join in gathering berries and edible greens. Siddhartha listened carefully to the monk's explanations of which foods were edible, how they were to be found, and how to dig for roots and tubers.

After they had eaten and taken their rest under a boa tree, Siddhartha's companion turned to him and eyed his monk-like garment. "A monk's only necessities are a robe, a bowl for alms, a razor, needle, water-strainer, and a belt to hold these accoutrements. Beyond this forest you will find a series of caves where holy Brahmins dwell with their disciples. If you go there, they will outfit you with your needs." With that, the monk rose to his feet and walked back into the forest and disappeared.

six

NEWLY ROBED, AND with his belt cinched round his waist, Siddhartha moved from the region of the caves onto a flat plain ringed by low-lying hills. In the distance could be seen a shepherd herding his flock of sheep and goats. They were moving in his direction, and Siddhartha noticed that one of the ewes was caring for two lambs, one healthy, that kept bounding ahead of her, and another that was lame and trying to keep up with the flock. The mother ewe was bleating miserably, while moving nervously between her baby lambs. Without hesitating, Siddhartha picked up the lame lamb and wound it round his neck. "Where are we going?" he asked the herdsman while falling into step.

"To the court of King Bimbassara," the herdsman replied.

When they arrived at the palace, Siddhartha stood aside and watched the shepherd drive his flock into one of the courtyards, where it was soon evident the animals were to be sacrificed. It was explained to Siddhartha by an onlooker that it was believed that the king's sins would be transferred to the animals upon their sacrificial death.

Siddhartha was appalled, and refused to relinquish the sheep he had been carrying on his shoulders. In the ensuing commotion, all eyes turned to Siddhartha, and the king, raising his hand, called for silence, for he could see in this young monk's demeanor and bearing that he was of a princely caste, and not an ordinary wandering mendicant.

The king waved the crowd into silence, giving the young stranger permission to speak.

"All life is sacred," Siddhartha began. "Think you that the Lord favors one aspect of creation more favorable than another, that one creature in His eyes is favored over another. Isn't all creation one in divinity, but with each a different part to play?

"All life wants to live. Who are we, mortal creatures, that we can sacrifice what we have not made and in defiance of the Maker. If we do not create life, we cannot take life. We should instead be guardians of our brother creatures, not heartless masters who exploit them to create false doctrines and creeds. For the greatest of all is the servant of all."

King Bimbassara was deeply moved by the stranger's words. He came down from the sacrificial alter and addressed Siddhartha, "I have been admonished for some time from the Brahmins and others to quit these sacrifices. Slowly, I have come to see the truth of their arguments, but until this moment I could not find a way to extricate myself from this accustomed ritual. From this day forward there will be no more sacrificial offerings, for I now see that we do not honor our Lord in this manner, but rather demean ourselves in His eyes. For in attempting selfishly to be more than we are, we have become less than we could be."

Having said this much, the king took his unexpected guest aside and spoke to him in private. "Tell me who you are and where you come from," the king implored.

"I am Prince Siddhartha of the Gautama clan in Kapilavastu. My father is Suddhodana, King of the Shakyans."

"I knew at once that you were a noble, and so your words did not surprise me. I do not know what brings you here in the guise of a wandering monk, but if you will stay with us I will lay my army at your feet and together we will rule this land. With your obvious wisdom and strength of purpose, our territories will grow and our kingdom will prosper."

"I am honored by your words," Siddhartha said, "however, it is not my aim to conquer and possess, to own more of what is perishable, or to have my work seen by men. All this I could have had, and did have, and left behind. The enemy I must conquer is sickness, old age, and death, and when I do I will have my kingdom."

"I can see by your resolve that what has been impossible for all others may be possible for you. Should you triumph over these tyrants, promise me you will return to Rajagrha and enlighten me with your Dhamma."

seven

THE KING HAD led a tortured existence since his son had fled the palace gates. At the urging of his wife, he once again sought the counsel of his Brahmins.

Said the chief Brahmin, "I understand now why Siddhartha was born a prince, with all the privileges, promises, and seductions of the throne. And further why he married well, and even had a son. For if a man is destined to embark on a great mission, great too must be the obstacles and obstructions, for only then can he be tested. In conquering these obstacles, he slowly acquires the strength to see his mission through. You will one day see your son again," he said, looking upward at the king, "but you may not recognize him when you do."

Siddhartha had crossed the Ganges River, and, passing through its eastern valley, he entered the northerly spur of the Vindhya Mountains. He was guided by three bold peaks that rose above the morning clouds as if reaching for heaven itself. In the forests beyond the valed city of Vaishali, he found the teacher he sought, Alara Kalama, who lived with his disciples in the caverned hills above the forest floor.

"I am a wandering monk who has yet to find a practice." Siddhartha had just spoken his first words to the Master Kalama, who studied his subject without speaking. Siddhartha continued. "Please teach me your doctrine."

"What is it you wish to know?"

"I wish to escape from the revolving wheel of sickness, old age and death."

"To do this, you must move beyond the world of the senses. I will explain my doctrine to you, but it is useful only as a guide to your own experience. By applying yourself to the teaching through meditative practice, you will come to understand the doctrine."

It wasn't long before Siddhartha had learned the doctrine in great detail and was able to answer all the questions correctly. Through one-pointed concentration he was able to enter the space inside himself where he was temporarily free of the distractions of the senses.

"Now you must move beyond the opposing worlds of yes and no, the tyranny of the mind that always judges but can never resolve its own dualistic dilemma."

"What of the endless repetition of desires that keeps us enraptured? I find myself moving constantly from one desire to the next."

"This is how it is when we are imprisoned in the phenomenal world, where we create dramas that do not exist, that are the product of our imaginary fantasies. The problem is not just our restlessness and our attachments, because if we are not careful we can become attached to our non-attachments."

"Where does this lead, then?" Siddhartha asked.

"To the realm of non-existence."

By watching his thoughts during meditation, Siddhartha began to see that his thoughts rose and fell, and by breaking his attachment to them he was able to achieve the joy of concentrated effort that also brought physical balance and well-being.

He explained his finding to Kalama, "This new joy I am feeling has slowly become an obstacle, or so it seems."

"That is correct. Joy is not the antidote to suffering. It too can become suffering if we stop there. What you must work for next is alertness and well-being."

Kalama had never before had a pupil like Siddhartha, for no sooner did he give him a new direction to move in, then the result was achieved by his pupil, along with the understanding that came about because each insight revealed a new experience of self.

"Well-being is not enough," Siddhartha was explaining.

"Yes," Kalama said, unable to suppress a smile and soft chuckle. "This is because you are now awake. You have achieved the four levels of meditative absorption and are no longer bound by your material form." Kalama looked up at Siddhartha and smiled again. "But there is more. You are not yet free of the cycle of suffering."

Kalama's teaching now moved into a new phase, but the more concentrated it became the harder Siddhartha worked, until, without realizing it, he had learned all that the Master could teach him.

"You have moved from "boundless space" to the consciousness that is able to perceive this, and that is also, finally, able to let it go. Your realization is now as great as mine. I have nothing more to give you."

Siddhartha demurred at his Master's offer to stay with him and pass on what he had learned and become, knowing that he had not yet attained enlightenment.

Once again Siddhartha was alone but joined to his path, that now carried him in an easterly direction. There was joy in his heart, and sadness, for he was leaving the place of his first liberation, and he was leaving behind his first teacher.

While on his way he heard of another teacher, not far distant, by the name of Udraka. When he presented himself to the Master, he explained what he had received from his former teacher, and also what he was searching for. Udraka had achieved a new level of meditation that he called 'Neither Perception Nor Nonperception.' Siddhartha set himself to learn what this meant, working with all his might and with the will he had developed under his first teacher's tutelage.

When Siddhartha had achieved the freedom inherent in this practice, Udraka, like Kalama, assured his pupil that he had no more to teach him, and he, too, asked Siddhartha to remain with him and take leadership over his community of monks. Siddhartha refused, explaining that although he was able to stand beyond the space occupied by form and formlessness, he knew that the witness that could watch was not free but must remain and enter again the cycle of suffering in its next rebirth. "Therefore," Siddhartha told Udraka, "I have not yet achieved enlightenment. My goal is yet before me."

As Siddhartha traveled about the country, he began to observe the ascetics who had committed themselves to self-denial by way of a strict discipline that each of them had worked out for himself. Some thought they could achieve enlightenment through the limiting of food-intake, bordering on starvation, others immersed themselves in cold streams and rivers during the winter months, or sat naked before blazing fires, enduring flames that blistered their flesh; some took up their abode in regions where corpses had been abandoned, where they also took a code of silence. And still others tried to live on grasses alone, behaving for better or worse like the sacred cows they admired.

After crossing the Nairanjana River, Siddhartha ascended Mount Gaya and came to a forested region near the village of Sena, in the Uruvilva district. He settled himself there and began to devise his own austerities in pursuit of enlightenment.

Siddhartha's past experiences had shown him that he could not achieve his goal by studying with acknowledged masters, for they had taken him as far as they could; he would have to master himself and evolve a teaching based solely on his own experience and understanding.

In the quiet village of Sena, along the banks of the river Nairanjana, in the shade of its towering trees, he found a place propitious and inviting where he could begin the next phase of his work for liberation.

eight

A S HE BEGAN to fathom the purposes of the ascetic life, Siddhartha saw, too, that his way would be different from that of the other ascetics, for it was clear that each of those he had observed sought deliverance for themselves alone: some to avoid unfavorable karma; others to avoid rebirth on the earthly plane.

It was their detachment from life that troubled Siddhartha, and he asked himself how the ascetics differed from those involved in ceremonial rites and in the doing of various good work for the purpose of emancipation through mental discipline.

If the seeker were to be of service to anyone, Siddhartha thought, wouldn't he first need to perfect himself through self-knowledge? If life was calamitous, didn't this calamity arise from the defective nature of each being, and wasn't it from there that the journey must begin? "What I seek for mankind," Siddhartha reasoned, "I seek first for myself. But really, there is no difference: I am mankind, and mankind is me. I must therefore purify myself."

Moving through the wilds alone, Siddhartha came face to face with his fears. Unfamiliar noises terrified him: the sounds of animals unknown to him, the snapping of a branch, the far-off rumble of thunder—all these made him tremble and want to run away.

He began visiting forest shrines at night, which filled him with terror and dread, but by standing firm and facing each fear as it arose in his mind, he began slowly to conquer this weakness in himself. By doing so, he saw that fear was perhaps his and man's greatest enemy, for it undermined hope and faith, as well as a healthy belief in oneself.

The greatest fear, he realized, was that of one's own death. Once he had conquered this in himself, he felt he could endure anything in pursuit of his aim.

Having recognized that the discursive mind is the enemy of the spirit, he devised an exercise for working on this problem. He began by clenching his teeth and pressing his tongue against the roof of his mouth, believing that in this way he could suppress his thoughts until his mind crumbled. He was attempting to use his mind to control his mind. But apart from strengthening his will, he saw that he was powerless to control or even subdue his thoughts.

But little by little, a certain mental clarity began to appear.

Next he attempted to arrive at a state in his meditations where his breathing had virtually stopped, but the result was a loud roaring in his ears, and severe head pains. Although his mind was temporarily stilled by this practice, he could not endure the pain in his body.

He began to be more successful with his experiments when he realized that each was a product of his questing spirit and questioning mind, and in each case he arrived at a clarity that was unique to his nature, that was practical, realistic, and down-to-earth. He knew that truth in action was above truth in thought, and therefore each experience provided him with the data he needed to fulfill his quest. He became more and more thorough in his experiments for all of these reasons.

News of Gautama, as he was now known, began to spread, for it was said that he had equaled his master's conscious attainments yet he had refused to share in the training of their adepts, instead striking out on his own to lead an ascetic life, determined to reach enlightenment. The monks and ascetics came to observe him from a distance, and it was they who gave him the name Gautama, after his clan, for he was now no longer Siddhartha but one of them— and yet not of them—for they sensed that he would one day achieve nirvana.

Among the seekers who came out of their own curiosity and need was the Brahmin Kaundinya who had attended the prince's name-giving ceremony, predicting at the time that Siddhartha would one day achieve Buddhahood. Kaundinya was now a homeless mendicant as well, and with his fellow seekers, called the Band of Five, that included Vashpa, Mahanama, Ashvajit, and Bhadrika, had journeyed to Uruvilva to become Gautama's disciples, imitating his austerities in the hope of achieving enlightenment for themselves.

"I am now practicing submission of the flesh," Gautama explained to his followers. When I began this practice some time ago, I decided I would eat in a day only what I could hold in the hollow of my hand: a few peas, beans, lentils, or rice, or at most a single crabapple."

Gautama had grown so frail from this practice that his followers began to tend to his immediate needs, while also following his lead.

Six years had passed since Gautama had left his home to become a wandering monk, but the enlightenment he sought seemed as far away, if not further away than when he had first set foot on the path. By now, because of the mortifications to his flesh, he began to resemble an old man, with withered skin and falling hair, who had to be helped when he walked. His spinal column began to resemble a string of beads, his buttocks two camel hooves, his head a shrunken gourd, while his eyes, having faded into their sockets, began to resemble two distant stars in a reflecting well.

One day, while struggling to reach the river's edge to bathe himself, he stumbled from exhaustion, unable to rise from the ground, until he grasped an overhanging branch that had mercifully bent down to help him to his feet.

Gautama struggled as best he could until he reached the base of a banyan tree above the river's bank and sat down in great pain and bewilderment. At that moment he remembered the peaceful bliss he had experienced in his youth, sitting under the rose-apple tree, safely exploring with his mind that was at rest in the bosom of nature. Reflecting on that moment, he realized that the spirit cannot be tyrannized into freedom through the mortification of the flesh. "The spirit is free. It has always been free, it is this other, this self that is not free—that I have not set free but have placed into a deeper bondage instead. The body is my vehicle, but how can it help carry me to my goal if it has become a broken vessel?"

His revelation was answered by the smile of eternal grace. For at that very moment there appeared in the presence of Gautama a young woman named Sujata, who had vowed to the Tree-Spirit he was sitting under that upon the birth of her longed-for child she would make noble offerings to the tree every year. She bowed before Gautama and offered him the rice and milk porridge she had prepared, believing he was the keeper of the tree's spirit.

Sitting on the opposite bank, the Band of Five were appalled to see their teacher eating substantial food. "Look," they said to each other, "he is eating householder's food and has given up the struggle for enlightenment." Without another word, they got to their feet and began to wander off in the direction of Benares.

Gautama, nourished from the porridge, fell into a deep reverie and did not even notice their departure.

The next phase of his quest had now begun to take hold in his mind. He realized that in order to continue his journey he would need to bring his body into balance with his mind, thereby restoring his spirit. He began eating again in a normal way, taking his begging bowl into Uruvela, where he was once again in the presence of everyday people. Gradually, his health began to return, and with it his powers of reason. He thought, "There is a pattern to our lives that we cannot see but must live, and in living fulfill the destiny of its design." But he could not yet see that he had to arrive at the border of death and to the depths of despair before he would be able to reach the heights he aspired to, for one could not be experienced without the other. He had become the equal of death, and of life. His six-year ordeal in the wilderness had been completed. And now, at the age of thirty-five, with all of his bridges burned, as naked as a newborn child and even more alone, he was about to enter his final transcendence.

nine

WITH HIS STRENGTH renewed, and calm
in spirit, Gautama again made his ritual climb up Mount Pragbodhi
to the cave in which he took his meditations. One day, the quaking
of the earth rendered the cave too dangerous for sitting, and as
Gautama began descending the mountain a heavenly voice whispered, "There is a Diamond Seat beneath a bodhi tree southwest of
here across the Nairanjana River."

With no more instruction than that, he set his foot upon the
path that would lead him to the mentioned tree, not knowing that
his life would soon be changed forever.

Standing before the bodhi tree, Gautama peered through its
tangle of branches into its cavernous shade, and although he had
forgotten about the "Diamond Seat" mentioned in the heavenly instructions, he saw that he was meant to find his place here and seek

the enlightenment that he had long sought and that now seemed to have been claimed for him from above.

Gautama was startled to hear the singing voice of a boy carrying a basket of sweet grass on his back. "What are you called?" Gautama asked the boy.

"Svastika," the boy answered.

"Good fortune!" Gautama exclaimed, for that was the meaning of the boy's name. "May I have a bundle of your sweet grass to make a seat for myself?"

The boy happily obliged and, resuming his singing, continued on his way.

Gautama moved through the tangled vines of the bodhi tree, and, facing east, he took his customary lotus position, sitting on the mat made from the grass he had been given. Closing his eyes, he vowed that he would not again rise from this spot, even at the cost of death, until he had attained supreme and absolute wisdom.

As expected, Gautama's resolve materialized the diaphanous form of Mara, who projected his demons, creating through the powers of illusion projections of power through acts of war, the pleasures of the senses through seductive dancing girls, and pure reason through the achievements and allure of the intellect. But Gautama, because of his long, arduous struggle with his own weaknesses, had, in overcoming his fears, defeated his own demons until he had arrived at the brink of complete self-realization. He made quick work of Mara, who knew now that his tenure had been permanently broken by the coming Buddha.

Gautama went deeper and deeper into himself until he reached a state of perfect selflessness. He could feel the moon rise in the evening sky and the night grow silent as he entered the first level of meditation. He began to travel back into and through his former lives, viewing them with the calm disinterest of non-attachment, seeing that birth alone is the cause of old age, sickness, and death.

In seeing all things in himself, and himself in all things, he realized that this life in all its stages is but an outward appearance of but one aspect of existence, and is not, in itself, a true reality. It is for this reason that the illusion of birth leads inevitably to the illusion of death. Therefore, the source of suffering is the false belief in permanence as well as the belief in the existence of separate selves. This is ignorance. Understanding is the key to liberation; to be in the present moment, to simultaneously see, clearly and plainly, all that exists inside and outside of oneself, is to be aware of the oneness of life. Anger, greed, hate, doubt, jealousy, hubris, and fear are all founded in ignorance. This ignorance causes us to live in the world of duality; to understand this will ultimately negate the cycles of birth-death. Since everything is in flux, there is neither breathing in nor breathing out; there is only breath, and breath is beyond time— for we are breathed into existence on this plane and at our last out-breath we enter the next plane of existence.

To see is to love, to love is to understand, to understand is to transcend the ignorance that binds.

Now an image came to Gautama the Buddha as a proof of his transcendence. From being seen, "The House Builder," as he called it, had been routed. "You shall not build that house again," he said, addressing his former self. "Your rafters of pain have been dismantled, and your ridge pole of delusion is demolished. My mind has now attained the unformed nirvana, and reached the end of every craving, of being and non-being alike."

ten

HE HAD SEEN. He had become. He was.
In realizing his Buddhahood, he saw that he was the latest in a line
of succession of Buddhas who had seen the truth and were now
obliged to teach it. He saw, too, that the truth was one and percep-
tible because it existed openly, yet remained hidden to man because
of his ignorance. But the method of teaching this truth was given
ever anew because as the wheel of humanity turns, the method of
bringing mankind into the light changes. And the truth must be
modified to fit the time as well as the station of each individual who
seeks the truth.

After seven days, the Buddha rose from the Diamond Throne
at the foot of the bodhi tree and began walking round and round,
circling the tree under which he had received his release from the

bondage of this world, thinking how he was to pass on what he knew for the good of mankind. He wandered to a nearby banyan tree and sat beneath its shade and began to reason with himself about his task, for he saw that he could not give out the teaching in its purest truth, for man was fettered by his passions and consumed by his bodily functions, and habits, and needs. And so he pondered how he was to teach them that they were not their bodies and that it was this illusion that kept them imprisoned in their ignorance.

Another seven days passed, with thunder appearing on the horizon and casting a great rain storm over the land. But Buddha did not move from his spot because he knew its cause was Mara. A voice descended from the rain-swollen clouds, saying, "Do not be deceived, true liberation can only be achieved by ascetic practices. You have wandered from the truth."

"I am realized," the Buddha answered. "I am going forward, not back where you came from, Mara, for I know with clarity who you are. Come out from your hiding place and look me in the eye." But Mara, vanquished again, quickly retreated.

The rain stopped and a great silence pervaded the land. The doubts that had assailed the Buddha were now replaced by the God Sahampati, who descended out of the clear blue transcendence of morning. Bowing before the Buddha, Sahampati entreated him to formulate a new method for the teaching of the eternal truth he had received, explaining with encouragement that there were those who could understand and who were eager to receive the Dhamma.

Soon after the God Sahampati disappeared, an image appeared in the mind of the Buddha of a forest pool in which the lotus grows with its roots in the mud. He thought, "All grow in mud but all do not reach the surface of the water, yet of all those that do not, all are able to open their petals. But there are always some that flower in great splendor and ride serene in their glory upon the living stream.

"Since everything strives for the light, understanding is possible—for some more than others. The sun does not discriminate, but shines on all equally, though all do not equally grow.

"My task is before me then. I cannot slack in my effort. I have seen the truth and I must fully give of it, but carefully, and within the framework of a method that is understandable and practical, and that will fulfill the promise I see for it."

The Buddha was deep in thought when two merchants passing on the road found themselves drawn to the banyan tree. Having been guided by the Buddha's light, they made their obeisance and humbly offered him rice cake and honey. "Blessed One, please count us as followers who have come to you for refuge, for as long as breath may last."

Buddha was moved by their humility and sincere request, but he could see that they did not actually wish his instruction. He thought, "Perhaps they are a sign that my enlightenment is real and that it is my destiny to teach." When they had departed, he ate the rice cake and honey, breaking his long fast, and it was only then that he began to consider to whom he might first present his Dhamma. Almost at once he thought of Alara and Uddaka, his original teachers, but after deep concentration he saw that Alara had died seven days before, and Uddaka on the previous night. "What a great pity," he thought, for if either Alara or Uddaka had heard the Dhamma they would have soon understood and become fully realized.

Upon composing his thoughts again, he remembered his first followers, the monks of the Band of Five. He saw with his inner eye that they had taken themselves to Benares and were residing in Deer Park at Isipatana. "I will go there," Buddha said, and rising to his feet, he began the two hundred kilometer walk.

He had not journeyed far when he came upon a monk who introduced himself as Upaka. When he approached the Buddha, he said, "I can see at a glance that you have travelled far on the way. Who is your teacher and to what Dhamma do you subscribe?"

"I am self-realized," the Buddha answered. "Through my own efforts I have transcended. I am all-knowing, the Buddha, and I go now to set the Wheel of Dhamma in motion and to beat the deathless drum of immortality."

"All things are possible," Upaka said to the confident stranger, and, smiling to himself, continued on his way.

The Buddha was bemused, but on reflection he realized that the teaching cannot be given, but must be taken. It is the pupil that must be the active agent in the transmission of the Dhamma. Only when the pupil is ready can the teacher appear. "The monk Upaka refused the Dhamma because he didn't know the teaching existed, but once I have imposed the Dhamma on the world, it will never again be extinguished, but only transformed again and again into new forms by future Buddhas."

eleven

WHEN BUDDHA AT last reached Deer Park, he had no trouble finding the Band of Five. They saw him coming from a distance and said among themselves, "Here comes the self-indulgent one."

"Clearly he has given up on the ascetic path."

"We will not receive his bowl nor his outer robe."

"Let us not pay him homage or even rise up to greet him."

But as the Buddha drew closer their hearts began to warm and they recalled their fondness for the one who was once their leader.

When the Buddha reached the seated monks, they rose involuntarily to their feet and taking his bowl and outer robe, they prepared a seat for him. Then they brought him water and towel so he could wash his feet.

They felt calmed by his serenity and radiance, and yet the change in his being left them feeling uncertain about themselves. Not knowing how else to address him, they called him Friend, and by the name they knew him by, Gautama.

"Dear monks, I have returned as your Friend, and also as the Buddha. I am here to instruct you. By practicing as you are instructed, you will come to self-realization through direct knowledge, for this is the supreme goal of the holy life. It was for this purpose that you left the house life for the homeless life."

As the Band of Five stood before the Buddha, a great struggle ensued in their beings. They could see that their unwillingness to accept Gautama as the Buddha came from their own denial of the very thing they had spent their lives pursuing. But then, slowly, like the morning sun rising above the earth and warming it, the radiance from the Buddha's countenance opened their hearts to the truth of consciousness, calling into being their own highest parts.

They saw themselves in the Buddha and the Buddha in themselves.

At last the monks were convinced and began to prepare themselves to receive the Dhamma. Gautama fell silent, now trusting that in the stillness that followed they would come into accord with the deliverance that awaited them.

They had retired to a sheltered area where they began to meditate from late afternoon until nightfall. When they opened their eyes it was dark, and all around them was a pervading silence, and a light from the moon that was like a lamp above their heads. The Buddha was now ready, as were his disciples, for the turning of the Wheel of Dhamma for the first time.

The five monks gathered in a semi-circle around the Buddha. Before speaking, Buddha looked over his disciples one by one, holding each in his heart. They watched as he closed his eyes, slowly, and then opened them again, before speaking. "There are two extremes that are not to be cultivated, but rather avoided. These are: devotion to the pursuit of pleasure in sensual desires, which is low, coarse, vulgar, ignoble, and harmful; and second, there is self-mortification, which is itself painful, ignoble, and harmful."

Buddha paused while his disciples reflected upon the truth of his utterance, for they knew well that the Buddha had fully experienced the results of the behavior he had just condemned.

"Monks," Buddha continued, "I have found a Middle Way that avoids these two extremes. And it is this Way alone that gives vision and understanding, and leads to peace, to direct knowledge, and to enlightenment and nirvana."

"And what is the Middle Way, Lord?" Kaundinya implored.

"It is the Noble Eightfold Path, which is comprised of right view, right intention, right speech, right action, right livelihood, right effort, right mindfulness, and right concentration.

"This is the Noble Eightfold Path, but it is not complete without your understanding of the Four Noble Truths. First there is dukka, the Noble Truth of Suffering: birth is suffering, aging is suffering, sickness is suffering, death is suffering, sorrow and lamentation, pain, grief, and despair are suffering, association with what is loathsome is suffering, disassociation from the loved is suffering, not to get what one wants is suffering. The second is the cause of dukka, which is called tanha, which is desire, or selfish craving; third, the overcoming of tanha; and the fourth, right effort, as the way out of the predicament of our captivity.

Buddha paused again that they might absorb what he had just given them, and again they saw his life in his word. But they also began to see in his words their own lives, and this was the beginning of their revelations into themselves and the words of truth.

They asked, "And what is the origin of this suffering?"

"The origin of this suffering is the second of the Four Noble Truths. It is craving, which produces renewal of being, and is accompanied by relish and lust, and out of this relishing comes craving or sensual desires—a craving for being, a craving for non-being."

The Buddha paused and judged the effect of his words on his disciples before continuing. "There is the Noble Truth of the cessation of suffering: it is the remainderless fading and ceasing, the giving up, relinquishing, letting go, and rejecting of the same craving. And the way to this is the Noble Eightfold Path that I have already told you of, which is right view, right intention, right speech, right action, right livelihood, right effort, right mindfulness, and right concentration."

The Wheel had been turned, the Dhamma delivered, and a sense of peace and quietude and rest came over the gathering, while the Buddha reflected on the moment, before continuing his talk. "I did not achieve enlightenment—that is to say, the vision, the light, and the truth—until I had fully penetrated this suffering in myself, and then the origin of this suffering in myself. For it was only then that

I was able to penetrate, finally, the truth of the cessation of suffering in myself. It was then that I found The Way."

A long silence ensued, after which the Buddha looked over his disciples again, each in turn, and when his gaze fell on Kaundinya he knew that his teaching had been fully received.

Meeting the Buddha's gaze, Kaundinya declared, "Lord, I see for myself that all arising is subject to cessation. I know this to be true because of my own knowledge of myself that your words have delivered me to."

"Kaundinya knows!" the Buddha exclaimed, "Kaundinya knows!" And from that day forward, the venerable one became known as Annata Kaundinya, or Kaundinya Knows.

Kaundinya asked that he be fully ordained as a disciple of the Buddha, and the Buddha said, "Come forward monks, the Dhamma is well proclaimed." And, placing his hands on Kaundinya's crown, he continued, "Live the holy life for the complete ending of suffering," and with that simple declaration, the ordination was completed.

The Buddha remained in Deer Park, teaching the Dhamma to his immediate disciples and all others who became attracted to his teaching, and before long, the remaining four monks of the Band of Five were fully ordained, having themselves become enlightened by the Dhamma of the Buddha.

It was time for the Buddha to expound the teaching of nonself, in contradistinction to the central tenet of Hinduism, that believed man's soul or eternal self transmigrated from rebirth to rebirth.

Speaking to The Band of Five, he said, "This self, contained by our material form, is not real but an illusion, for if it were real it could not lead to affliction. Therefore, feeling is not self, perception is not self, consciousness is not self, and above all, these our bodies are not self. It is like the monkey who clings to each branch before swinging to another. Can he call any of these branches his self, this mode of travel being, this not-so-solid air a solid self? I ask you, monks, is material form permanent or impermanent?"

"Impermanent, Lord," the monks answered in unison.

"Consider your feelings. Are they not, like the body, ever changing, controlled by our moods, the weather, our welfare, and so on. And our thoughts, are they not also, like our feelings, in constant flux. Where there is no center, no stable point, can there be a self? These are the factors that control our perceptions and consciousness, which are also ever changing, and all these are moored to a body that declines, fades away, and perishes."

The Buddha again asked, "Is what is impermanent pleasant or unpleasant?"

"Unpleasant, Lord."

"Can we therefore call what is impermanent, unpleasant, and subject to change what I am? Can I call this a self, or say that this is me?"

"No, Lord."

"Seeing this, we become dispassionate toward material form, toward feeling, perception, consciousness, and all the formations of the mind. And when we become dispassionate, lust fades away and the heart becomes liberated, and with its liberation comes the understanding of this illusion of self, which was dependent on our clinging to these five aggregates.

"And with this understanding comes the end of suffering."

twelve

IN NEARBY BENARES, the young son of a rich merchant awoke in the pre-dawn after an evening of sensual indulgence, feeling hung over and weary. Stumbling out of his chambers, he came upon the sleeping bodies of the maidens who had just hours before entertained him with their music and dance. His eyes moved over the disarrayed forms that seemed to him a mockery of the pleasures they had earlier provided; one with her hair unfastened, another with an arm slung over a drum, a third with a tabor under her chin, and a fourth with her lute turned over. He noted spittle forming at the corner of one of their mouths, and beside her, the very one who had delighted him with her playing, with her beautiful instrument now tilted awkwardly under her arm.

He hurried through the door and out into the night. He was gaudily dressed in his evening raiment, in which he had slept, and still wearing his golden slippers. Moaning under his breath from the remorse he felt, he seemed fully aware for the first time that his life was empty and without meaning.

His flight carried him to Deer Park. With the first light of day breaking against the horizon, he saw a lone figure, that of the Buddha, pacing slowly against a row of hedges, apparently deep in thought. The forlorn prince could be heard muttering, over and over, "Horror, horror."

The Buddha approached the young prince and, taking him by the arm, walked him to a nearby bench, while asking him his name.

"I am Yasha," the prince replied, "I have walked here from Varanasi."

"I know," Buddha said, for he had no trouble seeing himself in the young prince, and understood the nature of his suffering. He placed a hand on his shoulder and lectured him quietly about the false self and its illusory pleasures. Yasha was too confused to take in what the Buddha was saying, but he was comforted by his presence and felt a healing beginning to take place inside himself. His mind began to clear. He found himself relaxing, and it was then that he began to absorb the teaching, which fell on him as effortlessly as plain cloth soaking up dye.

Yasha's mother was alarmed by his disappearance and sent her servants looking for him, not knowing that her husband had already begun to trace the prints of his golden slippers in the sand that eventually carried him to the entrance of Deer Park.

When Yasha saw his father in the distance he became alarmed, knowing he would have to return to the palace. The Buddha understood at once, and said, "Quick, take refuge behind this bush and I will see what your father wants."

When Kulika drew near the Buddha, he could feel, because of his own spiritual nature, that he was in the presence of a holy man. "My Lord," he said, "I am looking for my son whose footprints have led me to this park."

The Buddha put his hand on Kulika's shoulder. "Sit here beside me, perhaps he will soon appear." Sensing that the king was ripe for the Dhamma, he began to preach to him in a way that was understandable in terms of the king's experiences and the yearnings of his soul, all of which were immediately discernable to the Buddha.

After a time, Kulika said, "Blessed One, you have made the Dhamma clear, righting the overthrown, revealing the hidden, and showing the way to one who has been lost; all this by holding the lamp up to the dark, for these eyes to see the visible forms. I take refuge in the Dhamma."

Hearing his father's words, Yasha became liberated, and when he appeared from behind the hedge, the Buddha knew that he was no longer capable of returning to his former life.

Yasha's father was relieved to see his son again. "Quick, Yasha," he said, "you must return home at once, your mother is beside herself with worry."

Buddha understood that Kulika, unlike his own father, was a man who understood the needs of the spirit. "Wait," he commanded Kulika, "I ask you, if your son has seen himself as he really is, can he go back to the life of sensual pleasures he knew, clinging to the perishable, now that he has understood the nature of life and the cause of his own suffering?"

Kulika hesitated, and then, drawing himself up, declared, "If Yasha will resolve to follow the path you have marked out for him, it will be a great gain."

Yasha embraced his father and, turning to the Buddha, said, "I wish to be ordained."

"It is done, Yasha," Buddha said. "The Dhamma is well proclaimed. Lead the holy life for the complete end of suffering."

thirteen

BUDDHA COULD NOT have known that with the ordination of Yasha his teaching would not only change his entire life but would eventually change the life of his nation as well.

The news had spread fast among the leading merchant families of Benares that the clansman Yasha had shaved off his hair and beard, put on a yellow robe, and gone off to a life of homelessness as a follower of the coming forth of the Buddha. "This can be no ordinary Dhamma, for Yasha to have done this," they said. When they came to speak to Yasha, he took them to the Buddha, whose instructions quickly liberated their hearts, and they too were ordained.

Soon there were sixty-one Arahats in the world. The responsibility for his work had taken a turn, and Buddha was faced with a new decision. Calling his followers before him, he said, "Monks, I am free from all shackles, whether human or divine. You too are free from all shackles, whether human or divine. Therefore, you must each go now across the land out of compassion for the world and teach the Dhamma that is good in the beginning, good in the middle, and good in the end. Promulgate the holy life for all to hear. Brush the dust of sleep from the eyes of those who are not completely asleep and have eyes with which to see. Some will understand, others will not. Do not be troubled by this, only persist, remembering that you fulfill your mission for the sake of the peace and happiness of the world."

As time went on, the wandering monks began to bring in those who wished to be ordained into the order. As a result, Buddha saw the necessity to delegate certain duties. Calling his Arahats before him, he said, "I have decided to authorize our monks to give ordination to our lay brothers in whatever quarter or country they may be found. This may be done by following a simple procedure: first, the hair and beard should be shaved off. Then the yellow robe put on, with the upper robe arranged on one shoulder, and homage paid at the monk's feet. Then, after kneeling, with hands out, palms pressed together, they should say three times: I take refuge in the Buddha, I take refuge in the Dhamma, I take refuge in the Sangha."

The Buddha had gone off toward Benares for his retreat during the rainy season, with the intention of travelling to Uruvela, for he had not forgotten his promise to King Bimbassara.

Traveling alone, with his wooden staff and bowl, the Buddha, having passed through a wooded area, took his rest at the base of a pipal tree. Until now all of his thoughts had been absorbed by his quest for enlightenment, and although it had been his intention all along to free men from the slavery of the illusions by which men run their lives, he had never considered what would happen if his Dhamma were to be accepted and formulated into a teaching that his practitioners would help promulgate. "I am not a priest, or a king, or a man who can fit himself into an organization of any type, much less be expected to run such an institution. Already, my monks begin to band together, building shelters of permanence, while I wander, alone, free and unadorned. Isn't this the life I proclaimed long ago? Is there any reason now to abandon it? Can I not teach wherever I find myself, and is the salvation of one worth less than the salvation of many? Can I not begin each day from where I am? Are not the needs of each day meaning and burden and blessing enough?"

The noise of a party close by broke into his thoughts. Thirty men of privilege were having a picnic in the woods with their wives. One of the men, who was unmarried, had brought a courtesan along. While the party swam in a nearby pond, the courtesan stole off with their jewelry, and it was the commotion that ensued that disturbed Buddha's thoughts.

Soon the men came crashing through the underbrush and were surprised to see the Buddha, serene and composed, sitting beneath a tree at the edge of the woods from which they had just emerged.

Catching their breath, they asked, "Venerable One, have you seen a woman passing this way?"

The Buddha answered that he had not, but asked the men, "Why are you chasing after a woman in this fashion? Is it better for you to seek another or to seek yourselves?"

"To seek after ourselves, I suppose," they answered.

"Sit here beside me, then, and I will instruct you in the Dhamma."

They knew at once that they were in the presence of a Holy One who radiated kindness, stability, and strength. After prostrating themselves, they took their places around the Buddha. Before introducing the Dhamma, he tested them with simple exhortations about duty, generosity, and responsibility, after which he spoke to them about compassion and forgiveness. It wasn't long before the immaculate vision of the Dhamma arose in them. They, too, asked to be ordained, and the Buddha said to them, "The Dhamma is well proclaimed. Lead the holy life for the complete ending of suffering."

Continuing his journey to Uruvela, Buddha soon came into the domain of the matted-hair ascetics who were followers of the three brothers: Kassapa of Uruvela, Kassapa of the River, and Kassapa of Gaya. They were fire worshippers who prayed to Agni, the Vedic fire god, and in their numbers they totaled one thousand strong. The followers of this religion constituted the principal spiritual influence over the kingdom of Magadha.

They were in possession of supernatural powers and were therefore influential over their followers, which included King Bimbassara. Buddha knew that if he were to present his Dhamma to the king, he would first have to convert the three brothers, and that this could only be accomplished by entering into their belief system and exposing its limitations in the light of his own perfected teaching.

It was early evening when Buddha called at the hermitage of Uruvela-Kassapa, asking if he might stay the night. To dissuade the Buddha, who was clearly a holy man but of a persuasion that was noticeably different from theirs, Uruvela-Kassapa explained that the only available chamber was the cave, in which their sacred fire was enshrined.

"A royal serpent occupies this cave as guardian of the fire. He is ferocious, venomous, and will surely kill you if you enter his chamber."

This was exactly what the Buddha hoped for, but as Uruvela-Kassapa did not wish for the Holy One's death, he refused at first the Buddha's request. It was only after the Buddha begged for the third time that Uruvela-Kassapa relented and granted his permission.

Although the serpent remained hidden when Buddha entered the chamber, the serpent was aware of his presence, and also clearly aware of the Buddha's fearlessness.

The Buddha placed his mat in the center of the chamber and assumed his meditation posture. The serpent produced a cloud of smoke, hoping to chase the Buddha out, but the Buddha responded with his own, even greater cloud of smoke. The serpent countered with fire, and the Buddha responded in kind until the chamber became an inferno of blazing fire and billowing smoke.

The matted-hair ascetics gathered outside, and said, "Poor blessed monk of the handsome face and brave countenance. He is surely going to be destroyed by the royal serpent."

But when morning came, Buddha emerged from the charred interior with his bowl in hand. When Kassapa approached through the crowd, the Buddha said, "Here is your serpent, reduced to size, and coiled harmlessly inside my begging bowl."

Kassapa was taken aback, but concealing his amazement, he acknowledged that the Great Monk was in possession of supernormal powers. But, he concluded to himself, he is not an Arahat like me.

Buddha took his leave and went to live in a nearby wood. That evening, the Four Divine Kings appeared before him, illuminating the woods, and after paying homage they assumed their protective positions at the four quarters.

When Kassapa came in the morning to invite the Blessed One for their morning meal, he asked what it was that had come to the woods in the night, lighting up the sky.

Buddha said, "They were the Divine Kings of the Four Quarters, who came to me to hear the Dhamma."

Kassapa thought, "The Great Monk is even mightier than I thought if the Divine Kings came to him to hear the Dhamma. Nevertheless, he is not an Arahat like me."

It happened that Kassapa's annual sacrificial ceremony had come due, and all of his followers from the surrounding area had arrived, bringing large quantities and varieties of food for the Grand Feast.

Kassapa thought to himself, "If the Great Monk attends and performs one of his supernormal feats before my people, his renown is bound to increase and mine to diminish. If only he were not to come."

But the Buddha had read his mind, so when the morning of the Great Feast and Sacrifice arrived, he took his begging bowl and walked to Lake Anotatta in the Himalayan foothills.

When the ceremonial evening had passed and Kassapa next encountered the Buddha, he asked, pretending disappointment, "Why did the Great Monk not appear for the grand occasion?"

The Buddha told him, matter of factly, that he knew his presence would disturb him, and so he stayed away.

Kassapa was even more shocked than before, and although he was speechless in front of the Buddha, he thought to himself, "The Great Monk is indeed mighty and powerful if he can read my mind, yet I know that he is not an Arahat like me."

Although Kassapa wished he had never met this mysterious being, he felt compelled once again to ask him to take his next meal with him in his private chamber. The Buddha accepted, saying to his host, "Go ahead and I will soon follow." When Kassapa had departed, Buddha traveled out of his body to a distant rose-apple tree, plucked its fruit and, arriving at the fire chamber, took his seat and waited for Kassapa to arrive.

This time Kassapa was truly distraught. Unable to contain himself, he sputtered, "How can this be. I left before you, but arrived after you?"

Buddha smiled and handed Kassapa the rose-apple he had

plucked, saying, "Have this rose-apple, whose scent is as wonderful as its color, and with a taste that exceeds both its color and its scent."

But Kassapa refused, saying coldly, "You brought it, you eat it," while thinking, "Whoever he is, he is not, nor can he be, nor will he ever be an Arahat like me."

"Enough!" Buddha exploded, "you will go on forever saying to yourself I am not an Arahat like you, when the truth is that you are not an Arahat at all. You are so full of yourself that you cannot see outside of yourself. Instead of offering charity and compassion, you are consumed with power and greed. You are not, nor have you ever been, nor will you ever be an Arahat if you continue on the path you have chosen."

The searing truth of Buddha's words awakened Kassapa, who knew now who the Great Monk really was, and, falling to his knees, said, "Lord, I wish to receive the going forth and full initiation from the Blessed One."

"You may speak for yourself," Buddha said, but not for your five hundred followers. They must be consulted first."

Kassapa went to his followers and announced his intention to lead the holy life under the Blessed One, saying, "You must each do as you see fit."

They answered, "We have known for some time who the Great Monk is, and if you have accepted him, we will do so ourselves."

Cutting off their matted locks and taking all their belongings, together with their graven images, they went to the river and cast them into the stream to be carried away. Then they went to the

Blessed One and prostrated themselves, asking to be initiated into his Dhamma.

Kassapa's brothers down river saw the matted locks, icons, and possessions of their brother's followers being washed away on the moving water. They rushed to their brother and asked, "Have you found a better way with the Great Monk?"

"Yes," Kassapa said, "his way is better than ours, he is the Great Teacher come to lead us into the light. Cast off your possessions and follow us who follow him."

fourteen

THE BUDDHA HAD first thought, "I will present the Dhamma, only that, and what follows will be good, and each successive step will be arranged for me by the steps I have taken—if they are taken in accordance with the truth, which they shall be." But now that his followers exceeded one thousand in number, he saw that his task was more complicated than he had thought.

As he set out now for Rajagriha with his new followers, he began to ponder how he was to enlighten the fire-worshipping converts who now constituted the bulk of his followers. To draw out the highest in them, he realized, they must first be purged of the impediments lodged deep in their minds that prevented clear thinking and being.

They had stopped briefly at Gayashirsha, a volcanic peak, from which they could see in the distance the Nairanja River and Mount Pragbodhi. "From these volcanic rocks we stand upon," Buddha said to his followers, "we can see our way ahead. But when we look out from where we are inside ourselves, we see that everything is burning. Whatever we see seems to be burning, whatever we hear we hear through burning ears, whatever we smell has a burning odor, whatever we taste with our burning tongues tastes burnt, and likewise, whatever we feel through our burning bodies has a burnt feeling. Our minds are burning and whatever we think seems to be burning."

Buddha continued, "These are the flames of illusion and super-stition that burn in us, through which we see the world not as it is but as we believe it to be because of the flames of ignorance and anger and covetousness and fear. When we liberate ourselves from these attachments, we will be free from the sufferings of this world."

As Gautama had hoped, the truth of his spontaneous parable on fire had penetrated the minds and the spirits of his new converts, and like clutched birds suddenly released into the air, their defilements flew from them into the vanishing ether.

Wandering through fields and villages, the yellow-robed monks attracted the curiosity of all those they passed, for a following such as the Buddha had created was something unknown in their land.

They reached Rajagaba, where they stopped at a shrine in the park named Sapling Grove. The news of their arrival soon reached King Bimbassara, who had never forgotten the young monk of the Sakyan clan. He announced to his inner court that they must go out to greet the Holy One. "If his followers number more than one thousand then we must go in equal numbers to pay our proper respects and to receive his Dhamma. I know that he has come to fulfill his promise to me, and will provide me with the fruits of his enlightenment; therefore, I will bring him my people, that all may benefit."

The Buddha was pleased to see the king and greeted him respectfully, pressing his palms together and bowing from the waist. The king, after making proper obeisance to the Master, took a seat at the Buddha's side. When the ceremonial greetings and blessings had been accomplished, and the great crowd had settled down, Buddha became aware of the thoughts of those who were questioning in their minds if the Great Monk was being led by Uruvela-Kassapa, or if, as it appeared, Uruvela-Kassapa had become a follower of the Great Monk, for it was plain to see that Uruvela-Kassapa had shaved his head and beard, and was now dressed in yellow robes like all the other adherents of Gautama the Buddha.

Addressing Kassapa, the Buddha said, "Please tell the gathering why it is you have abandoned your fire-worshipping religion."

Kassapa answered, "The sacrifices at the altar of the fire ceased to give me pleasure when I realized that there is a permanent place of peace and freedom beyond the senses."

"Yes," Buddha declared, "To dominate is to diminish, and to possess is to lose."

Kassapa rose from his seat and, prostrating himself before the Buddha, declared, "The Blessed One is my guide and I am his disciple."

A murmur passed through the crowded assembly, followed by

complete silence. The Magadhan were now ready to receive the Dhamma. Buddha began by speaking in a general way about the need for a moral life based on eternal principles, such as: Forgiveness, seeing the other in oneself, generosity and almsgiving, and also caring for one's neighbor. He concluded his litany by preaching the Dhamma of the Eightfold Path.

Before long, the spotless, immaculate vision of the Dhamma appeared to eleven of the twelve hosts of the Magadhan Brahmins and they became adherents.

At the same time, King Bimbassara found himself being initiated into the light of the Dhamma through his own objective experience of himself, and rising to his feet and facing the Buddha, he declared, both for the needs of his own being, as well as for all those in attendance, "My Lord, when I was a boy I made four wishes for myself: the first, to be a king one day; the second, that sometime in my life I would encounter a fully enlightened Arahat; the third, that in meeting the Blessed One, I would pay him honor; and the fourth, that in receiving the Dhamma I would understand it.

"Until today, only my first wish was granted, but now, in the course of this single afternoon, the remaining three wishes have been given unto me."

"Lord, I now have but one wish left, and that is to be received as a follower and to become a worthy adherent to your Dhamma for as long as my breath may last."

After he had spoken, King Bimbassara rose to his feet and— bowing before the Buddha with pressed palms—invited him to the palace in the morning to take his first meal of the day. The Buddha accepted in silence, as was his customary practice.

The following morning, Buddha arrived with his large following in tow. Carrying his bowl in hand, he walked down the palace hall to be greeted by the waiting king. The king's attendants, who had been waiting in anticipation to see The Blessed One, marveled at his beauty and grace, and each felt that his smile was a benediction of kindness that penetrated to their very being.

The king himself served the Buddha, and when the meal was finished and Buddha had put his bowl aside, king Bimbassara took the occasion to relieve himself of the thoughts that had been swirling inside his head during the night. He cleared his throat and with a look of satisfaction on his face, he began, "Lord, I have been wondering where the Blessed One will live with his monks, thinking that he would need a quiet and secluded place without disturbing sounds, hidden from view, not too far from town and therefore accessible to those who might seek him out." He stopped to look again at the Buddha, whose encouraging smile prompted him to go on. "It was then I realized that our own Bamboo Grove, that lies on the outskirts of town, has all the necessary qualities. I would like, therefore, to present the Bamboo Grove to the Blessed One.

When the Buddha graciously accepted, a golden pitcher was brought by one of the servants. While the king poured water from the pitcher over the Buddha's hands, he recited a formal ordination consecrating his donation.

fifteen

THE BAMBOO GROVE would become the first Buddhist Monastery, and from the very first day Gautama—putting aside all his doubts and misgivings about the leadership role he must assume—began to establish a program of conduct, along with guidelines and a curriculum for his monks to follow. He had earlier established the ordination ritual for receiving monks into the order, but there were other consideration now that he had an actual site for his work.

To begin, he determined that their robes had to be made out of discarded rags that had to be washed clean and then sewn together, before being dyed a uniform yellow. To be accepted into the order one had to be twenty years old, and have a sincere and honest wish to learn the Dhamma.

A monk's only possessions were a bowl, a razor to keep his head shaved, a needle, and a filter to strain his drinking water. After the monastery was built, each monk was provided with a narrow wooden bed, built just above the ground, to prevent him from crushing insects while sleeping.

Only one meal a day was allowed, and that before noon, and this was to be obtained by going from door to door begging scraps of food. Since the householder would acquire merit by giving food, the monk was to go for almsgiving to the poorest houses as well as to the richest. He was to stand modestly before a door or window, and if nothing was offered he was to move on quietly, not allowing any unkind thoughts to enter his mind. The Buddha explained, "Let the sage seek his food from house to house in the same way a bee takes honey from flowers, without hurt to scent or bloom."

The monks were not to notice if the woman giving them food was old or young, attractive or not, controlling his sense organs, so as not to be distracted by sounds and smells, or anything extraneous that would deter him from his goal.

When begging on the road, a monk had to be prepared to preach the Dhamma, using the Buddha's words that he had learned by heart.

Meditation was taught and practiced, leading to equanimity of spirit, and freedom from all craving, which would ultimately lead to detachment from the world. Not all would become enlightened Arahats, but one was never to relinquish one's struggle with Right Views and Right Effort, for it was the struggle with one's weaknesses that the Buddha prized above everything else.

At this time, two friends named Sariputta and Moggallana, who were spiritual brothers, having left their prominent families at an early age to seek enlightenment, were now part of a clan of wandering seekers totaling two hundred and fifty in number. Their teacher was of Sanjaya, one of only six acknowledged masters residing in India at that time. Realizing that the path they were on had taken them as far as they could go, and knowing it would not lead to the deathless state, they made a pact that if one of them should encounter an advanced master, he would tell the other. Sariputta, restless and ever on the lookout, happened one day to be begging alms in Rajagaha and saw a yellow robed monk walking nearby. Struck by the monk's serenity and poise, he began to follow him. After the monk had received his alms and had taken an inconspicuous seat in the park, Sariputta approached him and asked his name and the name of his master.

"My name is Vashpa, and my master is Gautama, the Blessed One, formerly of the Sakyan clan."

"You reside in the Bamboo Grove then," Sariputta said.

"Yes."

"I know of your master, but have heard nothing of his Dhamma. What does he teach?"

Vashpa had been a member of the Band of Five, the first convert to Gautama's teaching, but he did not say this to the stranger. Instead, he replied, "I am new to the teaching and can tell you very little."

"Can you sum up the teaching in a parable or expression of faith?"

"I will try, friend, to impart my understanding. The Blessed One has defined the cause of all things arising, and in each case he has said that their cause determines their cessation. To put it another way, just as everything that rises must fall, everything that begins must end."

Sariputta's understanding was instantly transformed, for he realized that whatever sense he might have of himself was subject to cessation, and that nirvana was therefore something beyond cause and effect, beginning and end, or any other formula or concept that the mind might conjure.

After thanking Vashpa and bowing before him to express his profound gratitude, Sariputta hurried off to tell his comrade of the great discovery he had made.

Mogallana, like his friend, was instantly converted, but when they told their teacher of their intention to join the monastery in Bamboo Grove, they were surprised by their teacher's response. He began to twitch and squirm, his face growing red with anger and disappointment. He felt rejected, and his only thought was that his two prized pupils were about to defect. "I have my position as a teacher to consider, and the fame it has brought me. I cannot abandon all that I have built up, and impose this new Dhamma upon myself and my following. In any case, whatever you may say about it, my Dhamma has been proven, and Gautama's has not."

Because he was their teacher they could not argue, but after they had made their plea three separate times and were refused, and since Sanjaya would not offer them his blessings, they respectfully withdrew from their master's presence. They felt obliged as leaders in their community to tell the other followers of their intended departure and of the Dhamma they had chosen to follow. They were surprised to find that their fellow monks were in agreement and eager to join them in their trek to the monastery in Bamboo Grove.

Gautama was directing the crew of worker monks framing the main structure of the monastery when he observed the two wandering ascetics and their entourage moving in his direction at a determined gait. With his all-seeing eye, Gautama recognized at once who they were, and turning to his disciples, he said, "Note the auspicious appearance of these two wanderers named Mogallana and Sariputta, for they will in time become my chief disciples."

sixteen

WORD OF GAUTAMA'S monastery in Bamboo Grove spread far and wide. Soon seekers from across India began to appear to hear the Blessed One's Dhamma and in many cases to receive ordination into the new brotherhood, that would soon become known as the first egalitarian monastery in India.

But as Gautama's teaching grew in strength and purpose, it was met by an equal force of resistance from the townspeople. "This monk Gautama is obliterating the clans and causing childlessness to occur by creating widows, as our men leave their homes to travel the path of this new Dhamma."

Soon the townspeople devised a stanza of derision with which to mock the monks they encountered on the roadways and in the towns, chanting:

Breaking the heart of Sanjaya
the monk, Gautama, led his band away;
now they descend upon us
whose heart will he break today?

But the Buddha bolstered the spirits of his monks, assuring them
that the disturbance would soon pass. "In seven days it will sub-
side. When people mock you with that stanza, you can reprove them
by chanting the following:

The Dhamma of the Great Ones
leads to enlightenment, not heresy
therefore look inside yourselves, not outside
for there you will find only jealousy

When the townspeople saw that they could not intimidate the
monks, they began to accept that they were being led by their
Dhamma, not deluded by it. The wisest among them began to ad-
vise the others that it was possible Gautama was a true master.

Gautama's first small victory was but a precursor of what was
to come, for when the time came to create an egalitarian sangha he
would be turning the political and social culture of his country on
its head. It was unheard of that people of all classes, castes, gen-
ders, and occupations could practice as equals the spiritual life. Not
only did ordinary soldiers flock to the Buddha, but landowners and
nobleman. For at that time in India the sage was considered the ideal

man, and those who were literate and well to do were pleased to follow Gautama, who was like them in that he had once been an aristocrat.

For those who embraced the teaching, there was no higher goal than attaining spiritual freedom from the bonds of illusion and suffering.

Gautama continued his travels, spreading his Dhamma through the lands of all the tribes—the Mallas, the Vajjis, the Koliyas, and others, but he avoided the territory of his own people, the Sakyan. Although he was known throughout the Ganges Valley as Sakyamuni, the Sage of the Sakyas, his own tribe had not seen him for seven years.

King Suddhodana, Gautama's father, had followed the fortunes of his son, and in his longing he wondered if they would ever meet again. I am growing old, he thought, and time, the merciless judge, will soon claim me. I must see my son before I die.

He called in one of his messengers, and confiding his longing, sent him on a mission to return with his son. "Tell him his father yearns for him, as the flowers of the field long for the rising sun."

But as time went by and the messenger did not return, he sent a second, and then a third, until a total of nine messengers had gone off, with none returning. Nor had any sent words of explanation to account for their mysterious disappearance.

Each messenger, having once seen the Buddha and hearing his words, forgot their mission and became initiated monks.

King Suddhodana was disconsolate but determined, and called in Udayin, the son of one of his ministers, a childhood friend of

Siddhartha, thinking that the sight of him might spur in his son a longing for home.

Udayin, like the others, was soon initiated into the order, but unlike his predecessors he did not forgot his mission. When the winter season had come to an end, Udayin knew that Gautama would soon renew his travels. He now approached Gautama for the first time, and with his permission, began reciting a long poem he had written in which he hinted at a father's longing for his son, of a land deprived of a healing Dhamma, without a sage to give it utterance. Gautama, having recognized and recalled with warmth his childhood friend, was moved by his thoughtful and subtle presentation. His words had sparked a longing in Gautama to see his father again, and he decided on the spot to pay a visit to the king's palace.

Gautama, accompanied by his Arahats, began the long journey. When at last they crossed the Rohini River, they began to notice that the houses were decorated with garlands and flowering branches in his honor. As they approached the city, they were told by a welcoming contingent that arrangements had been made for their stay in Banyan Park.

Children were sent ahead bearing flowers, and when the king arrived in sight of the encampment of monks, he stepped down from his palanquin and began walking slowly toward his son, who rose from his seat to greet his father.

When the king had moved close enough to Siddhartha to examine his features, he could see that this was no longer the son he remembered, but a living Buddha. He knew now that his son would never be his heir. Having understood this, the great denial he had long carried in his heart was instantly annihilated.

Gautama was aware of his father's revelation and embracing his father, said, "I know that your love for me has made you grieve, but if you can loosen this love that tightly binds and with its strands embrace all fellow beings, then you will know me at last for what I am."

Nothing more was said between father and son, and nothing more needed to be said. In that instant, King Suddhodana had realized the first of the four levels of enlightenment and in time would become a fully realized Arahat.

The following day, Gautama and his monks walked to the city to beg their food. The king had not thought to invite them to his palace, assuming an invitation was not necessary. But Gautama was no longer a prince but a follower of an older tradition, and as a member of his own calling he knew it was wrong to presume to any rights of privilege.

At the sight of the monks wandering through their streets, with Gautama among them, the townspeople began murmuring among themselves, for they could not comprehend what they were seeing. "The Prince is dressed in the robes of a monk and carries in his hand an earthen bowl for alms."

The king was alerted and made a request for Gautama and his followers to gather inside the palace walls where a banquet was being arranged in their honor. The king felt humiliated and admonished his son. "Our people feel disgraced seeing you begging in the streets."

"It is our custom to depend on people for our alms."

"But for them you are still of royal blood and it is not the custom of royalty to beg in the streets."

"I am no longer of your lineage, father. I am of the lineage of Buddhas."

The king understood, and bowing to the Buddha he took the bowl from his hand and led him with his retinue into the banquet hall.

When all had gathered at the dining table, Gautama received his relatives one by one. All were present but his wife, Yasodhara, who had been invited by her king but had refused. She had said, "If I am worthy of his regard he will come to me."

After they had eaten and Gautama had spoken to the gathering, he turned to his father and asked, "Where is Yasa, my wife?"

"She has refused to come, for she did not know if you would receive her."

Gautama rose to his feet and beckoning his closest disciples, Sariputta and Moggallana, went straight to her quarters, accompanied by his father. Before entering her chambers, Gautama instructed his disciples, for he feared that if Yasha attempted to embrace him Sariputta and Moggallana would interfere, for neither the Holy One nor his monks were allowed to touch or be touched by any woman.

"Although I am free," Gautama explained, "she may not be, and having longed for her husband her grief may be so great that she will need to embrace me. If this occurs do not interfere."

Gautama was shocked to see Yasha sitting in a corner, her hair severely cut, and dressed in sewn rags, like a mendicant. When she lifted her eyes to behold her husband she was overcome by the sight of him and fell, sobbing, at his feet.

Gautama placed his hand tenderly upon her head and began stroking her hair until she had gained control of herself and rose to her feet. When she saw the king she grew ashamed and slowly withdrew again to her corner seat.

The king apologized for the princess. "It is from her love that she grieves. When her prince departed and did not return she learned that he had shaved his head, and so she did likewise. The same with her outer garments, that she has sewn from gathered rags. As you eat from an earthen bowl but once a day, she does likewise, as you gave up wearing flowers and perfume, she has done the same. As your faithful wife, she has stayed by your side in the only way she knew how."

Gautama turned to Yasodhara, his wife, and lowered his voice that only she could hear. "Yasha, I understand your suffering; I, too, suffered when I knew I had to leave you. You have always been virtuous; again and again you have assisted me and over lifetimes traveled at my side and helped me to attain great merit. It is from your holy nature, as the result of former sacrifices, that you have desired to become the wife of the Buddha. This, then, is your karma. Therefore, accept now the spiritual inheritance that surrounds your grief and transforms it into a heavenly joy."

seventeen

SEVERAL DAYS HAD passed since the grand banquet in the palace. There was a palpable silence in the air since Gautama's arrival, and with it a sense of peace. Yasodhara had gone to her window and looking down she saw Gautama sitting beneath a banyan tree talking to his disciples. She called her son, Rahula, to her side. "Do you see that man there beneath the tree whose radiance is casting a golden glow? That is your father. Go and ask him for your inheritance."

"He is not my father," Rahula answered, "the king is my father."

"The king is your grandfather. That man, called Gautama, is your father. Go now and ask him for your inheritance."

Rahula was understandably disturbed because he did not understand what his inheritance might be. He knew that if he asked his mother she would not tell him. Putting on his cap, he walked to the door, and taking the stairs, descended onto the street.

Yasodhara watched her son from the window as he moved with great reluctance in the direction of the Buddha.

Gautama looked over at the young boy standing at his side, and although he knew who he was, he showed no sign of recognition.

"It is pleasant to stand in your shadow, Lord," Rahula said, but his father did not answer him. "I've come for my inheritance."

Gautama looked away and continued speaking to those nearest him. Then he rose to his feet and began walking back to his quarters in Banyan Park.

Rahula walked at his father's side, tugging at his cap and murmuring to himself. He began kicking at clods of dirt that stood in his path. From time to time he tugged at the sleeve of Gautama's robe and said, "Lord, I want my inheritance."

When they reached the park, Gautama turned to Sariuputta and said, "Ordain him."

In this simple manner the Buddha's son became an aspirant of his father.

A great sorrow overcame King Suddhodana when he learned what had happened. He rushed to the park and confronted Gautama. "When you abandoned us it caused me great pain, but now you mean to take the son whom you left in your place. This is more than I can bear. The loss of a son cuts through the skin straight to the marrow. And you, the son I lost, mean to take from me the son you left behind. Listen to my words and promise me you will never ordain a youngster without the permission of its mother and father."

Gautama instantly understood the truth of his father's words, and he formulated a rule in accordance with the king's request that would forever be retained by all the sanghas in his order. Yasodhara was pleased, knowing that her son's ordination would occur in good time.

Ananda, Gautama's cousin and closest friend from childhood, became a daily visitor at Banyan Park, spending hours on end with Gautama, walking through the park and sitting in meditation with Gautama on a secluded knoll above the bank of a serene, green water pond that was partially enclosed by a ring of fir trees. It became their favorite meeting place, where they shared their sentiments over the past and where Gautama slowly initiated Ananda into his Dhamma.

Ananda did not suspect at the time the important role he would assume in the Buddha's life. For he was destined not only to become one of the Buddha's most important disciples, but he would fulfill those functions and needs that no one else could provide—becoming again the true friend he had always been, as well as Gautama's confidant and secretary. Together they would travel the path ordained by the Buddha, and in playing his part, Ananda would realize his own destiny and the fruits of his karma.

Before his visit had ended, both Gautama's mother and wife, Yasodhara, were ordained as lay followers. With this act, two new words entered the vocabulary of Buddhism—upasaka, meaning male lay follower, and upasika, meaning female lay follower. At that time females were considered impure and a threat to man's religious studies. They were therefore not permitted to join religious communities. The major Indian religion at that time was Brahmanism, which made no effort to disseminate its teachings. The Brahmins alone, as members of the priestly caste, were responsible for its religious rites. Those of other castes prayed in private and were dependent on the priests to intercede for them in presenting prayers to their gods. The Shudras, who were slaves or laborers and belonged to the lowest caste, were not permitted to profess belief in Brahmanism.

The Buddha's approach to spirituality was therefore nothing short of revolutionary, and he soon became a threat to the existing order.

Ananda was not alone in leaving the Sakyan Clan in order to follow the Buddha. He was joined by many other nobles as well, who, convinced of the truth of Gautama's Dhamma, took on the yellow robes of the ordained monk. Devadatta, Gautama's cousin and childhood rival, was among these, and Gautama knew that because of his self-centered nature he would provide inner work for others, while traveling the road of his own salvation.

One day Ananda confided to his friend and master that he thought the most forceful part of Gautama's being seemed to lie in his dual ability to be both expansive and flexible, so that giving and receiving seemed to him to be as natural as breathing was for everyone else.

"This is but my nature, Ananda, but people would like to copy what is part of my individuality, that is itself not necessarily a part of my teaching—for this that you speak of is not a condition of enlightenment. It is hard to make some understand that what is needed is for each person to become themselves. The model of the good life is to attain the highest in oneself—more than that one cannot do. This much in one life is all that anyone may ask of themselves."

Ananda looked puzzled and hoped that Gautama would say more.

"Of course there is more, but each stage must be fulfilled for the next stage to be possible. Ultimately, one's individuality must be given over for nirvana to occur, but before it can be given over it must first be acquired.

"There are many rivers leading into the sea, Ananda, but once the great ocean is reached, the names of the rivers disappear and we do not speak of them as such, we just say the sea."

"Is this not an argument then against Atman, the World Soul, which includes everything, the negative with the positive . . ."

"Just so, Ananda, but man is not included in that. A united harmonious universe does not include us because we have become lost."

"Lost?"

"Yes, just so, because of our ignorance. All else has been brought to a point by the laws of the universe, but man must bring himself to this point by himself. The potential for self-perfection exists, but it must be earned. And ignorance is our greatest enemy. We do not understand. It is as simple as this. Think what

I said, Ananda, every river does not reach the great sea."

"Is the sea the Atman then, the source of nirvana?" Ananda asked, but Gautama looked away, which was his habit when he had finished speaking on a topic. After a time he turned again to Ananda and said, "Each person must come to the truth in their own way, in their own time. The Noble Eightfold Path is more than a way, it is the guide that will accelerate the process of enlightenment."

eighteen

THE FIRST HEAVY-LADEN clouds of the rainy season had blown against the southern tier of the Himalayas. The three-month-long season of the monsoon had begun.

Throughout this time the growing army of monks continued to roam the land, begging alms and spreading the Dhamma. Tramping the grasses in their rain-soaked garments they were perceived as a nuisance to some of the townspeople, and they were criticized as well by the Brahmins who accused them of killing the life forms that lay beneath their feet.

Gautama soon found it necessary to observe a period of retreat during the rainy season. But in solving one problem he had created another, for in isolating his monks in protective areas other problems began to occur, which would become evident in time.

The rainy season passed, but the problem of settling his followers had not yet been resolved.

A rich merchant from Rajagriha who frequently passed through Bamboo Grove on his solitary walks had become enamored of the monks because of their grace and humility, and also their seeming detachment from the defilements of life. One day, he approached a gathering of monks at the river's edge while they were cleaning their begging bowls. "Blessed followers of the Buddha, please may I ask you where you take your rest at nightfall, now that the rainy season has passed and you are permitted to travel again?"

Looking up at the familiar figure of the man from Rajagriha, they assumed a posture of respect before answering the merchant's question. "We live out in the open, in jungle thickets, hillside caves, or when caves cannot be found, under overhanging rocks, and at other times under the blessed shade of trees."

The merchant fell silent, and began looking out over the still water. "Tell me," he asked, "if I were to build shelters for you, would you occupy them?"

"The Blessed One has not allowed shelters, but we will ask him if you like."

The next day the monk who had last spoken to the merchant approached him in the park with the news that the Buddha had given his permission.

The merchant bowed before the monk. "Please thank the Buddha for allowing me the privilege of service."

The Buddha knows that you are a man of religion," the monk answered. "I will tell him."

"I will build sixty separate dwellings, after which I would like to invite the Buddha and his retinue for a meal at my home to make the presentation."

On the evening before the presentation was to be made, the merchant's brother-in-law, a traveling businessman named Sudatta, returned home after a lengthy absence. Upon witnessing the elaborate arrangements that were being made, he asked, "Are these arrangements for King Bimbassara?"

The merchant laughed. "If it was but the king, I would not be so nervous. We are expecting the Blessed One, the Buddha."

Sudatta looked at him in disbelief. "Did you say the Buddha?"

"Yes, I said the Buddha."

Sudatta was dumbstruck. "Do you know what you are saying, that a fully enlightened being, sent from above, has appeared before us?"

"Yes, it is the Buddha."

"I must go to him then. I must see the Buddha."

"Now is not the time. Tomorrow is soon enough. One does not seek out the Buddha in the dark of night."

Sudatta reluctantly assented and retired to his home. But he could not sleep. Three times he was awakened in the night, thinking the day had dawned. At the third awakening he went out into the dark and began walking toward the city walls. When he reached the gate, it mysteriously opened by itself to let him through. But when it closed behind him he was seized by a sudden horror of the unknown, and a fear he had never known before gripped his heart and stopped him in his tracks.

A disembodied voice appeared in the dark. "Not a hundred noble elephants, not a hundred jeweled horses, nor yet a hundred beautiful virgins are worth so much as the tiniest step that needs to be taken now. Go forward! Go forward! Now or never more."

Three times the disembodied voice echoed its message in the dark, and with the third utterance the darkness lifted in obedience to the light, and Sudatta took one step forward, and then another. Moving forward now with effortless ease, he soon found himself in the Bamboo Grove, where he saw the Buddha seated beneath a mangrove tree. He realized without knowing how he knew that the mat beside the Buddha was meant for him.

"Come, Sudatta," Buddha said, "your seat has been made ready."

He knows my name, Sudatta thought, and with that all of his fears suddenly vanished. He prostrated himself before the Buddha. Not knowing what else to say, he asked, "I trust the Buddha slept well?"

"He sleeps in bliss who is at peace, Sudatta," the Buddha said. "The same things that prevent our sleep, prevent our peaceful going forth in life—and these are our sensual desires. Only when we are we free of our attachments, can we see that our existence is not separate. Only then is the mind free. That is why I say to you, he sleeps in bliss who is at peace."

Sudatta said, "I have been waiting since I was a little boy for this day to come, and now it is here, but I can hardly believe it is true. I take refuge in the Buddha. I wish only to be of service, Lord, in whatever way I can be used."

"Finding our way we come to this, Suddatta, and it is through this life and our participation in it that we find our service. Tomorrow, when we take our meal together, we can talk more. Now you must return to your home and reflect on everything that has been said tonight."

The next morning Gautama dressed and, taking his outer robe, with bowl in hand, he led the walk to the merchant's home.

Sudatta served the Buddha and his monks with his own hands. When the Buddha had finished eating and put his bowl away, Sudatta took a seat at his side. "Lord, if you will consent, I wish to build a monastery in Shravasti for you and your monks, where you may dwell during the next rainy season."

The Buddha nodded his approval and smiled upon Sudatta. "A person who possesses riches and uses them wisely provides a blessing upon his fellow man. I know that you have struggled with yourself, wishing to join us as a monk in the religious life, but it is better for you to continue with the work you know and love. The Dhamma has entered your life. If you are diligent, it will stay with you and serve you for the rest of your days. If we give, Sudatta, we must take; if we take, then we are obliged to give. You have found a way to serve, now you will be served in return. Wherever I am, wherever you are, when you turn to me I will be there."

Sudatta was a man of real wealth and influence who was capable of achieving whatever he set his mind to. Arriving in Shravasti, he began looking for a suitable location for a monastery, one that would have open spaces, running water, and with a location close enough to the city that the monks could seek their daily alms.

None of the places he examined seemed appropriate until he visited Prince Jeta's Pleasure Park. He knew at once that here he had found the perfect site. He made his proposal to Prince Jeta, but the prince only laughed, for he had no intention of selling his beloved park. When Sudatta insisted, Prince Jeta chuckled, and dismissed the offer by saying, "Very well, Sudatta, cover the entire park with gold coins and it is yours."

When Suddatta had amassed the necessary coins, and presented them to the prince, Jeta exclaimed, "Come now, Sudatta, you knew that my proposal was only in jest and that I had no intention of selling my precious park to you for any price."

But Sudatta insisted, and they argued until their confrontation turned into a legal dispute that was brought to arbitration in the local court. The mediators concluded that a price had been established and when that price was met the agreement was binding and the transaction therefore concluded.

Sudatta carried one hundred thousand gold coins in carts and covered the entire acreage, but for the entrance area at the park's gate. Prince Jeta by this time had come to terms with the agreement, and when he learned that the park was to be donated to the Lord Buddha, he said, "I will cover the entrance with gold of my own."

Sudatta was pleased, thinking that the prince's gesture would be a good omen for the park since a man of his stature, in sanctioning the retreat, would favorably influence the townspeople toward the sangha.

Without delay, Sudatta saw to the construction of the monastery that would be comprised of quarters for the monks, storerooms, service halls, kitchens, fireplaces for cooking and for heat, wells and well rooms, promenades, bathing rooms, dressing rooms, a pool and pavilions, terraces, and walkways.

It was not completed until Sudatta had exhausted his entire wealth. But when he stepped back and looked at his creation, he thought, "For once I have done something that is not for profit, and for which I need not even be thanked. This alone of all the things I have done can be exchanged for real merit, for only rewards such as this can be taken beyond this world."

The rainy season had passed and the roadways had opened again for the wandering monks who had not found a place for themselves in one or another of the monasteries that were beginning to spring up across the landscape of India.

Gautama's father, King Suddhodana, had grown seriously ill. Gautama knew, upon learning of his father's illness, that the end was near. With little time to spare, he travelled to his father's side to comfort and care for him, and to prepare him for the life that was to come.

The king opened his eyes to see his son seated at his side. He clasped Gautama's hand. "How quickly life passes, Siddhartha. It seems a day or two ago that I witnessed your birth and childhood. Now here you are, grown beyond me, but once again at my side." He looked away from his son and remembered again the great turmoil his birth had brought into his life. When he turned back and looked up at his son, his face bore a serene expression of contentment. "When I thought you would be a great warrior and you turned away, I did not see that you became the greatest warrior of all. When I thought you would be a ruler of our people and you turned away, I did not see that you would be a ruler not of our people only, but of our nation and beyond. When I thought you would not become a great monarch, you became a monarch and more, a ruler and more, a warrior and more. All the Brahmins were right, only they did not see that there was but one path you could take, not two, and that the inevitable journey had been made in Heaven, where your mother now rests and where I soon will go. Because of you I have received my greatest reward, my own Awakening. So different from what I dreamed you would bring, and so much more than any gift I thought that you or this world could provide."

nineteen

GAUTAMA SPENT THE ninth rainy sea-
son after his enlightenment in a Sangha on the Yamuna River in the
country of the Vatsans. Petty quarrels and arguments among the
monks had long since become a feature of monastery life, despite
the warnings and admonitions of the Buddha.

It came about that one of the monks was apparently guilty of a
minor infringement, that of leaving a bowl of unused washing water in the latrine. The accuser was a specialist in the codes of behavior that ruled the Sangha. By insisting on their strict observance, he
managed to inflate his importance to the community. The accused
monk, on the other hand, was a specialist in the Discourses, who
considered his function and importance to the Sangha to be on a

higher plane than that of the enforcer of rules. When his accuser asked him if he left the bowl of water in the latrine and he admitted that he had, he was told that it was an offense. "However," said the specialist in rules of conduct, "if you did not know it was an infringement of the rules, then there is no offense."

The specialist in Discourses said that since it was not his intention to sidestep the rules, he agreed that there was no infringement of the rules, and so the matter was closed.

It might have ended there, but the Discipline expert gossiped to his pupils that the Discourse expert did not know the rules. The pupils, in turn, gossiped to others that they considered the Discourse expert had committed an offense in that he said first that he was guilty but then that he was absolved because of his ignorance of the rules. He is a liar, they said, and therefore deserves to be suspended.

As a result of all this wrangling and pettiness, a schism occurred in the Sangha, with one party and its followers suspending the accused monk, and with the defending party refusing to abide by the suspension.

A monk who was not caught up in the hysterical bickering went to the Buddha, who was residing in a neighboring Sangha, and explained what had happened, and asked that he intervene.

After listening to everything the monk had to say, Gautama replied in anger, "There will be a schism in the Sangha, there will be a schism in the Sangha," and without another word he got up from his seat and went straightaway to those that had suspended the accused monk.

When he had convened the meeting and a seat had been made

ready for him, Gautama delivered a stern and determined speech. "Do not imagine that you can suspend one of your own for such a reason as this. Because of your hysteria over this matter, you have lost sight of the bigger picture. If this is allowed, a schism will occur in the Sangha that will soon be followed by acts of dissension."

A respectful silence followed, and when no one else rose to speak, Gautama got up from his seat and went directly to members of the opposing camp. Again, a seat was prepared for him and a long silence observed before he spoke to the assembled gathering. "We must all understand the importance of making amends for any offense we might commit, even if the act was committed out of ignorance and without any intention of causing harm. We do this out of regard for others, as well as from our respect of the laws that are there for each of us and are made for our protection and to deepen our understanding of the truth, but not as a device to punish one another through our narrow interpretation of the rules. Remember that our conduct is based on compassion, not enmity. By acknowledging the offense out of faith in his fellow monks, the accused avoids a schism in the Sangha."

The quarreling continued until it seemed the Sangha would explode in violence. Once again, the conciliation-seeking monk came to the Buddha and asked for his intervention.

This time, the Buddha commanded that all parties appear in the Great Hall. When they assembled, there was such a feeling of violence and agitation in the atmosphere that the Buddha felt himself unable to take his seat. "Enough, monks!" he exclaimed. "I say to you, no more quarrels, no more brawling, no more wrangling, no more disputing. Let it end here and now. I will not speak again on this subject."

There was a long silence before the monk who was a leader of one of the legations rose and addressed the Buddha. "Lord, let the Blessed One be at peace with this and not concern himself over this matter."

The Buddha could see that they were obsessed and that it was impossible for them to see the meaning and consequences of their misbegotten deeds.

On the following morning, after Gautama had wandered for alms and returned to his room, he said to Ananda, "When the mob raises its voice in unison, none think themselves a fool. Now that the order has been split, none think, 'I took part in this.' Their speech is no longer wise, for their minds are obsessed with words alone, and bawling at will, their minds uncurbed, with reason blown to the winds, none knows any longer what they do."

Ananda did not know how to reply. Wishing to soften Gautama's pain, he said, "They do not know what they do. They are like children without a guiding parent."

Gautama did not acknowledge Ananda's words, but continued as if he had not been interrupted. "They think only, 'he abused me, he hurt me, he offended me.' Enmity is never appeased by enmity. Only amity can appease enmity. This is an ancient principle that they have yet to learn. In such matters restraint is necessary, only then will quarrels cease."

"Even crooks and robbers have learned to act in accord," Ananda offered, "surely we can do as well as they."

A hint of a smile appeared on Gautama's lips, but disappeared when he spoke. "If you cannot find worthy companions, be like the king who leaves a vanquished kingdom, like a bull elephant that walks alone in the wild. For it is better that than to abide in the fellowship of fools."

Abiding by his own advice, Gautama removed himself from the Sangha and went into the jungle to be alone and contemplate. In time, the unruly monks came to their senses and, in order to restore peace in the Sangha, they resolved their dispute through confession and forgiveness, and once again there was peace and equanimity among the Buddha's followers.

Gautama was now residing at Jeta's Grove. His son, Rahula, had turned eighteen. One morning, they set out together toward the city for alms. Rahula, who had never tasted life, began to daydream and was in the midst of an elaborate fantasy he had concocted in which his father was the chief monarch of India, as had once been predicted for Siddhartha, had he chosen a secular path.

Gautama had been reading his son's mind, and turning to him, he said, "The life of material forms is like the stuff of dreams—whether inside of you or out, whether fine or coarse, or of superior of inferior quality, whether in the future or in the remembrance of the past—and nothing of this this can be said to be you. This is not what you are. You must never say of these dreams or theories of existence that this is my self."

Rahula withdrew in shame, and sitting under a nearby tree, he crossed his legs and attempted to meditate. Following behind, the venerable Sariputta came upon Rahula and sensed his troubled state. "Rahula, practice mindfulness of breathing, for if that is maintained, being will be developed, and this will bring great fruit and blessings."

That evening, Rahula returned to Jeta's Grove and joining his father, he asked of the Blessed One how he might maintain mindfulness in breathing in order to attain great fruit and many blessings.

Gautama replied, "You must become like earth, air, fire, and water. For whatever enters their space is absorbed, blown away, burned, or carried away, bringing neither shame, humiliation, or disgust to their elemental nature. Replace negativity with loving kindness, cruelty with compassion, apathy with sympathy, resentment with equanimity. Further, you must contemplate what is loathsome in the body in order to get rid of lust. And finally, you must contemplate your own impermanence to rid yourself of the conceit, 'I am.' By practicing mindfulness of breathing in this way, your being will grow, and in this you will find great fruit and many blessings."

twenty

GAUTAMA PASSED THE following rainy season at Veranja with a retinue of five hundred monks. There was a famine in Veranja at this time, and its citizens had been issued food tickets. Gautama learned that a family of horse dealers had also taken up residence in Veranja for the rainy season. When he heard that their horses, like his monks, numbered five hundred, he considered it a good omen and sent Ananda to speak to their leader. It transpired that the horse traders were aware of the Buddha's presence in Veranja and told Ananda that they felt honored to be residing in the same vicinity as the Holy One. They eagerly offered from their horse's stable a measure of bran each day for the monks.

Having returned with food for the order, Ananda was busy grinding up a portion of the bran on a stone for his Master.

Gautama called to Ananda from inside his dwelling place. "What is that sound of mortar I am hearing?"

"I am grinding horse fodder for the Blessed One," Ananda answered.

"Good, Ananda, you have done well. For this food we give our prayers, knowing that some day people will look down on even the finest rice cooked with meat."

Gautama was residing in Jeta's Grove when he learned that a murderer was living in that region of Savitthi, who went by the name of Angulimala, or Finger Necklace. Angulimala was a cold-blooded vicious marauder who terrorized the entire district with his wanton destruction of human life and property. He was fond of making necklaces from the fingers of his victims, and it was from this practice that he had earned his nickname.

Having learned of his whereabouts, Gautama set out on the road that would take him into the vicinity where Angulimala was said to reside. Although the road had been nearly abandoned by the villagers, from time to time Gautama came upon a lone traveler or scavenger living by the side of the road, and in each instance he was warned not to go on. "Blessed monk, bands of men in groups of ten, twenty, and even forty have traveled this road in pursuit of Finger Necklace and none have come back. No doubt their fingers are now dangling from Angulimala's neck."

Gautama thanked them for their concerns and quietly continued on his way. It wasn't long before he came in sight of Angulimala, who was crouched behind a boulder, believing that he was out of sight. Unable to contain his excitement, he began shouting out loud, "What a marvel, what a delight. Bands of armed men have come marching up this walk, and here we have an unarmed monk, fearless, foolish, and embarked on his final folly."

Rattling his sword, he leapt out from behind his boulder, but to his amazement Gautama walked passed him without either breaking his stride or hurrying his step. "How can this be, I have chased down and killed elephants and deer, and even a speeding chariot is no match for me, and here is this monk rushing ahead of me while walking at his normal pace."

Seeing he could not overtake Gautama, he stopped and shouted, "Stop, monk, stop!"

"I *have* stopped, Angulimala. It is not I but you who must stop."

Angulimala thought, "These Sakyan monks are known to speak the truth, so what am I to make of these words. He says he stopped while he has not, and he says I must stop when I have already done so."

"Angulimala," Gautama continued, "I have foresworn violence against all living beings, while you wish to murder everything that comes under your sight. This is how I mean that I have stopped and you have not."

The truth of Gautama's words stripped Angulimala at once of his armor of hate, and shaking himself like a dog who has emerged from a body of water, he was at once liberated from the haunting karma of his unconscious life.

"Come, monk," Gautama said, "and be my disciple on the Way."

With Angulimala at his side, it wasn't long before they reached Jeta's Grove. They were met by an angry crowd who had gathered at King Prasenajit's Castle. The king emerged from the crowd and met Gautama.

"What is the matter?" Gautama asked the king.

"Blessed One, my people are in an uproar because there is a killer on the loose in these parts by the name of Finger Necklace. He was last seen in your presence, and so it was feared you were dead. But here you are, alive, and it is Finger Necklace that has again disappeared. My people will not rest until he is caught and destroyed."

"What would you say," Gautama answered, "if you found this murderer with shaved head and beard, wearing a yellow robe, eating alms food once a day, and living the holy life, and with only goodness in his heart for his fellow man?"

"Why, we would give him food and lodging and protection. But we are not talking about a monk now, we are speaking of a notorious murdering fiend."

Gautama turned, and motioning towards the venerable Angulimala, he said to King Prasenajit, "Here is the one you speak of, this is Angulimala."

The king was speechless and began trembling with fear.

"Do not be afraid," Gautama said, smiling reassuringly at the king. "There is nothing for you to fear."

The king shook his head in wonder and walked with Gautama to his residence. When they had been comfortably seated, the king gave formal thanks to the Buddha for the miracle he had just witnessed. "It is a marvel and a wonder how the Buddha subdues the unsubduable, extinguishes the unextinguishable, and conquers without weapons that which cannot be conquered with weapons."

Gautama accepted with grace the king's words of thanks and accepted for himself and Angulimala the next day's meal at the palace.

Gautama continued to instruct Angulimala in the Dhamma while they remained in Jeta's Grove, for he was pleased by his progress, knowing that as he traveled through his darkest hours, he would need the comforting solace and encouragement of the Buddha so as not to lose his way.

One day, while Angulimala was moving through the streets of the town for alms, a large stone came out of nowhere and struck him on the neck. He continued walking without complaint, even though he could feel the blood trickling down his back. Soon a branch fell from a tree and came crashing down on his shoulder. Before he could distinguish what it was that had fallen on him, a pot fell down from a second story balcony and crashed upon his head, knocking him to the ground.

Gautama met him on his return and examined his torn and bloody robe and his blood-smeared face. "Now you have experienced the consequences of past acts. Because of your efforts, they have ripened early. If intentionally perceived in the light of consciousness, many lifetimes of suffering can be averted. All this that you have seen and that I have now witnessed is good."

Angulimala pondered Gautama's words and from his under-

standing, earned from his personal experiences, he devised a verse
for himself so as not to forget.

> To have seen my recklessness
> Is to be reckless no more.
> Now the full moon appears again,
> For the clouds have been dispersed.

> Who is it that can banish evil deeds
> And bring into being deeds of goodness,
> Making the full moon reappear,
> Formerly hidden by clouds now dispelled.

> A youthful monk devoted to the Buddha's Dhamma
> Shall light the world as the full moon lights the sky
> When clouds that masked them have been blown away.

twenty-one

THERE LIVED IN the city of Kapilavastu the wife of a rich merchant, named Krisa, whose young child had died, stricken with an incurable illness. Her devotion to her son was such that she was overcome with grief and refused to believe in the death of her child. Holding her boy in her arms, she entered the street and began knocking on every door, asking for medicine with which to restore his health, believing that he would again open his eyes and smile at the sight of her as he had done all the days of his young life.

One by one her neighbors turned her away, unable to provide the medicine she required.

At last she came upon a wise and sympathetic soul who advised her to go to Banyan Park. "There is a physician there who can cure every human illness. It is Gautama, the Buddha."

"You mean Prince Siddhartha," Krisa said. "I saw him when he first entered our street in his noble chariot and I remember that a verse expressing my joy fell from my lips. Yes, I will go to him. I see now what I knew then, that he is a a savior among men. He will open my child's eyes."

She approached the Buddha with a hesitant smile of hope on her lips, with her baby pressed tightly to her breast. The Buddha looked upon her with compassion and waited for her to speak. "Have you medicine for my child that will open his eyes again?"

"The medicine you seek can be found in town," Buddha answered. "Go at once and bring me a handful of mustard seed from the home of one of your neighbors, but only on the condition that death has not visited a single member of their extended household."

"I will go at once," Krisa said, with confidence, "and return with the handful of mustard seed."

Each of the families that Krisa visited took pity on her and eagerly offered her the mustard seed she asked for, but when she asked if anyone in their family had passed from them into the shadow of death, they all answered that at least one member of their family had died. Going from house to house, Krisa at last realized that death was not a stranger, but a constant companion to all those that live.

Krisa found a bench in the park and laid her child down at her side. She looked out over the flickering lights of the city, and accepted for the first time the truth of her situation and the reality of her life. From feeling separated and lost, she felt a deep connection with all living beings, each of whom was destined one day to die.

While some monks grew restless and became agitated during the long rainy season, Ananda came to relish these long periods of internment for it brought him ever closer to the Buddha, who in turn enjoyed having his periods of silence interrupted by Ananda's questions.

One day, Gautama said to his companion of childhood, "What are you thinking, Ananda, for I can feel that with your enquiring mind you are trying to penetrate the impenetrable, to resolve the unresolvable, with the resolute intention of knowing the unknowable."

"With you, Lord, the unknowable is knowable, the unresolvable is resolvable, the impenetrable is the penetrable."

"So it must be for all who have a curious nature. To question is to plant seeds of knowing."

"Seeds planted in the Dhamma bring flowers of understanding, Lord."

"Some instantly, Ananda, some in season. Everything has its time."

"Yes, Lord, this is how it appears."

"What is your question, Ananda?"

"Lord, why is it that formerly, when there were fewer training rules, did many monks achieve Arahatship, and now when we have even more rules, are fewer and fewer monks becoming Arahats?"

"It is a law, Ananda, that when beings degenerate the Good Dhamma disappears and as a result more laws must be instituted, but with fewer results. Conversely, when the counterfeit of the Good Dhamma disappears, the Good Dhamma reappears. In the same way, gold does not disappear from the world until counterfeit gold appears. It is not flood, fire, or wind that take gold away, but rather the appearance of misguided men.

"It is good that you have seen this, for the Good Dhamma does not disappear at once, like a ship lost at sea, but gradually over time, through the perniciousness of men, who are intent on taking, not giving. The True Dhamma is about service."

"How can we know when this happens?"

"There are five evil constructs that lead to the disappearance of the Good Dhamma. They are as follows: when the monks become disrespectful and contemptuous of the teacher, the Dhamma, the Sangha, the Training, and lose a resolute adherence to the goal.

"Now Ananda, no more questions until you have worked out for yourself the meaning of all that I have now told you."

While residing at Savatthi in Eastern Park, Gautama would often sit by himself on the porch outside the gatehouse watching the evening sun set behind the distant hills. On occasion he would be visited by King Pasenadi, the brother-in-law of King Bimbassara. King Pasenadi governed the great kingdom that stretched from the bank of the Ganges to the foothills of the Himalayas. When visiting the Buddha, he would often sit in silence to one side, just to be in the presence of the Holy One.

It was on such an evening that there passed before them seven naked ascetics, seven Niganthas, seven matted-hair ascetics, seven single-garment ascetics and seven wanderers with long hair and nails. Sensing that they were in the presence of the Buddha, they stopped, turned in his direction and began staring in silence. Seeing this, King Pasenadi came down from the porch and fell to one knee while pressing his palms together at his forehead. "Lords, I am Pasenadi, King of Kosala." After repeating this three times he rose to his feet and returned to the porch.

After taking his seat and seeing that the passing party had disappeared from sight, he asked the Buddha, "Lord, were any of those men Arahats, or on the way to becoming Arahats?"

"King Pasenadi, you are a layman living in the world of sensual pleasures, you wear garlands and perfume, and you deal in silver and gold. It is therefore difficult for you to know who among those who profess the spiritual life are Arahats or who will become Arahats. A man's character can be judged only if examined over a period of time and then only by one who has proper understanding. A man's purity as well as his understanding can be judged through careful discussion, and a man's fortitude will be revealed during times of adversity. But in all cases, these things take time and the full attention of a man with considerable understanding of such matters. How is this possible in the rush of daily life where such things are judged by external appearance, not inner content."

"Well put, Lord, your formulation expands and enlarges my own understanding. I have hired spies to work for me who turn out to be common robbers, and yet when they are cleaned up, bathed and scented, with their beards trimmed and dressed in white, they easily hide their inner worlds with outward manners and professed beliefs."

"It is true, a man cannot be judged by his appearance, for at a glance the unrestrained man easily resembles the man of discipline and principles. Those who are corrupt soon acquire a mask, for they understand the righteous better than the righteous understand them."

twenty-two

WHILE STAYING AT the Bamboo Grove near Ragagaha, Gautama met on his alms rounds a man by the name of Sijala. One day while walking through the park together, Sijala stopped and began performing a ritual in accordance with his religious practice.

He began by whirling in the direction of the four quarters, followed by a raising and then a lowering of his head.

When he finished, Gautama asked him why he performed this superstitious act. "I do it to ward off evil," Sijala replied. "I must protect my home and family from the demons. I am aware from your remark that you do not believe in such incantations, but let me tell you that this is how I pay my reverence to my father and how I keep his sacred name before me."

"It is to your credit that you perform this ceremony out of respect for your father, and to protect your home and family from the harmful influences of evil spirits; however, I can see that you do not understand the true meaning of the six directions.

"As your spiritual father, who loves you no less than did your parents, let me explain the true meaning of the six directions, for it is not enough to perform a superstitious ritual whose true meaning has been lost. When you turn to the East, it is to honor your parents, to the South to honor your teachers, to the West, your wife and children, then to the North, to honor your friends, and finally, when looking toward the zenith, you are acknowledging with reverence your spiritual guides, and then to the nadir point, all those that serve below you.

This is the religious service I would have you perform, for the purpose of this ceremony is to remind you of your duties."

Sijala had listened with rapturous attention to the words of Buddha. "You are right, Gautama, I never before knew what it was I was practicing, trusting in the ritual instead of myself, believing that what I wanted could be done without true participation, simply by means of obedience and blind faith. I see now that I must take responsibility in a new way for my actions and my thoughts, and that my practice must become intentional if it is to have meaning."

Whenever Gautama arrived at a new monastery, he would make the rounds of the lodgings of the monks with Ananda at his side. It was on such a day that they found a monk deathly ill, lying in his own excrement.

Gautama bent down and stroking the monk's head asked him the nature of his illness.

"Dysentery, Lord," the monk gasped.

"Have you no one to look after you?'

"I have no one, Lord."

"But why do not the other monks look after you?"

"I am no longer of any use to them, Lord."

Gautama turned to Ananda. "Go fetch some water, soap, and towels."

When Ananda returned they washed the monk and lifted him onto his pallet.

Having cleaned the monk, Gautama began feeding him while Ananda went into the chambers and arranged for an open session with the Buddha.

When all had gathered, Gautama addressed the crowded assembly with a question. "Is there a sick monk among you, here in the Sangha?"

"Yes, Lord," they answered in unison.

"And what is his illness?"

"Dysentery, Lord."

"Is there anyone to look after this monk?"

There was a long silence before one of the monks volunteered that there was no one to look after the sick monk.

Staring at the monk who had spoken, Gautama asked again why this work was being neglected.

"He is no longer of any use to the Sangha, Lord, that is why he has not been looked after."

The expression on Gautama's face caused all the monks to lower their heads in shame. There was a long silence before Gautama spoke again. "You are here without a mother or father to look after you. You must therefore look after yourselves. Loving kindness is a practice to be fulfilled, not an idea to carry around in your heads. If we do not keep after our brother, who will keep after us? Am I not also my brother, is he not also me? Now we must make another rule for the Sangha. The responsibility for each monk's welfare must fall to his teacher, or his co-resident, or, if he is a teacher, to his pupil, or yet to the Sangha itself, which must be responsible for the care of any who become sick, infirm, or in need of care for any reason whatever. To neglect this solemn duty is an offense not only against the Sangha, but against humanity."

That evening, Gautama and Ananda were sitting outdoors with the others, receiving the first hint of a breeze moving through the hot still night. Oil lamps were burning at intervals across the grounds, like drops of liquid light in the pitch black night. Moths, in great numbers, were hurling themselves into the oil lamps and being instantly extinguished.

Ananda turned to Gautama. "I sense that you are troubled, Lord, because of the moths."

"Yes, Ananda, I was thinking of those who have lost the Middle Way, who, plunging themselves in the sense world go to extremes, like moths that fall into a burning flame."

The reports of his son Rahula's conduct were not always pleasing to Gautama. He therefore decided to visit his son at the first opportunity. It was being said of Rahula that he had allowed his tongue to run away with his temper, causing considerable mischief in the Sangha in which he was staying.

Rahula was overjoyed to see his father and did not suspect that the Buddha was about to impart a lesson when he obliged his son to bring him a basin of water for the washing of his feet.

After the task had been completed and Gautama was drying his feet, he said to Rahula, "Is this water in which you washed my feet now fit for drinking?"

Rahula frowned at his father. "Of course not, father, the water is now defiled."

"That is correct. Let us now consider your own situation. You are a son of the Buddha, your grandfather was a king, and although you are a monk, you are unable to control your tongue. Because of this you have defiled your mind."

Embarrassed by the truth of his father's statement, Rahula carried the basin of water away and poured it on the ground. When he returned, Gautama asked him if the basin was now fit for holding water to drink.

"No, father," Rahula answered, "the basin is also unclean."

"Exactly like yourself. You cannot conceal what is inside your yellow robe, nor can you represent what its appearance signifies as long as you are not clean inside."

Once again Rahula fell silent and watched as his father picked up the basin and began whirling it over his head. "Aren't you afraid I might drop your basin and break it?"

"No, Father, the basin is cheap and without any value."

"Consider yourself, Rahula, whirling from one transmigration to the next, your body made also from the same substance as this fragile vessel, and like you it too will one day turn to dust, and what then will the loss be to you or anyone else if you are to continue as you are?"

Rahula was filled with remorse, and in that instant, his conscience was pricked into wakefulness by the harsh but loving kindness of his father.

One day, walking alone on a dusty road between two neighboring Sanghas, Gautama stopped to repose himself beneath his favorite tree along that walk. At some distance behind him, the Brahmin Dona came upon the Buddha's footprints, and looking at them he seemed to fall into a partial trance. "These are not the footprints of a human," he muttered to himself, "for what I see is a thousand whirling wheels, their spokes and rims and hubs all complete, in a way that nothing has ever been completed in this life."

The Buddha, meanwhile, sitting in a lotus position beneath the banyan tree had entered into the deep chamber of himself, in harmony with his essence and the spheres. He sensed the approaching Brahman and opened his eyes to see him standing before him.

"Can it be that you are a god?" the Brahmin asked.

"No, Brahmin, I am not a god."

"A heavenly angel then?"

"No, Brahmin, not a heavenly angel."

"A spirit?"

"No, Brahmin."

"A human being?"

"I am none of these, Brahmin."

Beside himself, the Brahmin blurted, "What are you then?"

"Had I not removed my taints, Brahmin, I might have been a spirit, a heavenly angel, or a god. But appearing as a human being, I have cut these from me at their very root, and as when a palm tree when cut to its stump can never again send new shoots of growth, I am such as the lotus flower that is born in water and grows in water, yet stands above it, untouched by water. In this way I was born in the world, grew up in the world, and transcended the world. Think of me without definition or name, only as one who is enlightened."

On another occasion, while traveling across the countryside at the conclusion of the rainy season, Gautama was approached by a Brahmin, who, after making the appropriate salutations, asked a question concerning nirvana. "Lord, if it pleases you, may I ask how it is that many follow your instructions but not all become enlightened. Yet each recites the Dhamma when asked, and all believe in their understanding of it. Since nirvana exists, the way leading to it must also exist, and as you are its truest guide, how is it that all who follow you do not attain?"

"Good Brahmin, I will answer your question with a question. Are you familiar with the road to Rajagaha?"

"I am, Lord."

"Good. Now suppose you are residing in Ganga, from which

the town of Rajagaha is due south, and you are approached by a traveler who asks you the way to that town. Would you not point out the appropriate road and give him landmarks to look for, naming the villages he will pass through, the lakes and groves to be seen on the way, and so on? But then, despite your careful and detailed instructions, the traveler takes a wrong turn and begins traveling in a westerly direction and loses his way. Now a second man approaches you with the same request, and you give him identical instructions, and in due course he reaches Rajagaha.

"How are you to account for this? You have given the two men the same instructions, but one reaches Rajagaha and other one does not."

"What is it to me, Lord, all I did was point the way."

"And that is how it is with me. There is nirvana, there is a way to nirvana, and there is a guide pointing the way. The Perfect One knows the way, but the path for each is slightly different and must be traveled alone. Some get lost, others turn back, but worst of all are those who say they believe, and think they believe, but in truth are without faith and therefore without hope."

twenty-three

It WAS IN the Buddha's seventy-second year, or the thirty-seventh year after his enlightenment, that his life was threatened along with the peace of the Sangha. Devadatta had never relinquished his jealousy over his cousin's noble accomplishments. He had become in time a respected monk, but one who had forfeited his work for inner freedom in favor of the acquisition of supernormal powers. Seeing that he was not among Buddha's favored disciples, he decided to seek power outside of the Sangha. Moving single-mindedly toward his goal, he soon won the confidence of King Bimbassara's son, Prince Ajatasattu, the second most powerful man in Rajagaha.

Unlike Devadatta, the prince was weak-willed, and was therefore easily taken in by Devadatta's supernormal powers, and seeing an advantage for himself in their assumed friendship and alliance, he was quick to shower Devadatta with the privileges of his estate.

Devadatta grew more arrogant and conceited as his powers increased and it wasn't long before he became obsessed over his perceived role in the Sangha, thinking that the time had come for him to take over the Buddha's position. As this thought began to take command over his being, his supernormal powers vanished, but in his hubris he failed to make a connection between the two.

When the news of Devadatta's apparent defection from the Sangha and his unholy alliance with the prince reached the Gautama's ears, the Buddha was quick to calm the news-bearing monks, who were confused about their own feelings of Devadatta's new found wealth and renown. "Devadatta is lost," Buddha explained, "but the lost are often found. Hold thoughts of compassion for those who go astray and never begrudge or resent them for what they do. Just as when a dog grows fierce from having drawn blood from its victim, Devadatta's inner world will diminish as a result of his sensual appetites being satisfied. Pity, too, the prince, whose corrupt motives in all this will soon lead to his own destruction."

Devadatta meanwhile continued to lead a dual existence, pretending to live the life of the monk while residing outside the compound. One day, following a large assembly in the Great Hall, he approached the Buddha and, bowing before him, palms pressed together, said, "The Lord Buddha is now aged and the time has come for his retirement and rest. If you will turn over the Sangha to me, I will see that the transition is smooth and timely, to the great benefit of all."

The Buddha looked long and hard at his cousin before answering. "Put such thoughts away, Devadatta."

But instead of obeying the Buddha's command, Devadatta asked again, and after receiving the same response, he asked for the third time. The Buddha responded now in a voice that thundered through the hall, "I would not turn over the Sangha to my chief disciples, Sariputta and Moggallana, why would I turn it over to a wastrel like you?"

After the red-faced Devadatta had been dismissed, the Buddha made a formal declaration and disposition. "Devadatta was one kind of man before, now he is another. For the good of the Sangha we must divest ourselves of him in the eyes of the populace. In doing this we disclaim his actions and speech as being in any way representative or reflective of our order. He alone must be held responsible for his acts.

"Sariputta, you must make a formal denunciation of Devadatta in Rajagaha."

"Lord, the townspeople have heard me speak in favor of Devadatta on more than one occasion."

"And what you said of him in the past," Buddha asked, "was it true?"

"Yes, Lord."

"Then in denouncing him now, you also speak the truth."

Those among the townspeople who had been taken in by Devadatta's duplicity and ill-gotten gains were critical of Saraputta's strong words of denunciation, but others placed the Buddha's wisdom above the powers of state as represented by the prince, and stated that the Sangha was just in its rejection of the fallen monk.

Meanwhile, Devadatta, not to be undone by the Buddha's actions against him, went to the prince with another proposal. "In olden days, when men were not so long-lived, you would by now have inherited your father's throne. Why should you wait until his death to possess what should have been yours by now? Kill your father and become the king, and I will see to the Buddha's death and take his place as the ruler of the Sangha."

The prince had long since given up responsibility for his own thoughts and actions, and in trusting in the wisdom of Devadatta, had become his unwilling foil. Without so much as a second thought, he accepted the dagger provided by Devadatta, and strapping it to his thigh where it would be concealed by his knee-length coat, he slipped unnoticed into the inner court. The king's officers, noting something suspicious in his movements, arrested him, and in searching him they quickly found the dagger.

"What is this for?" they asked the prince.

"It is to kill my father with," the prince said in defiance.

"Who put you up to this?"

"The Lord Devadatta."

The officer closest to the prince slapped him to the ground, and pressing his face to the floor with his boot, declared to the others that the prince should be destroyed, along with Devadatta and all the monks.

But another officer declared just as vehemently that the monks should not be killed because they had done nothing wrong, and in any case Devadatta no longer represented the Sangha because he had been formally denounced and excommunicated.

The third officer to speak said that neither Devadatta, the monks, nor even the prince should be killed, but that the king should be informed, and the prince turned over to his father.

The third officer's suggestion prevailed, and they brought Prince Ajatasattu before his father, King Bimbassara. The wise king had felt that there was dissension among his officers and soon learned that his men were of three minds concerning his son's actions.

"Could it be more clear," he stormed at his men, "that the Buddha and his monks had nothing to do with this. Did they not denounce Devadatta in the town square?"

Without another word of explanation, he removed those officers from the payroll whose opinion it was that the prince, Devadatta, and the monks should be killed. Those officers who stated that the monks go free but that Devadatta and the prince be killed were demoted, while those who thought that none should be killed, and the prince turned over to the king, were promoted.

Dismissing his officers, he turned to his son and questioned him. "Why do you wish to kill me?" he asked.

"You have reigned long enough, the Kingdom should now be mine."

"Very well," the king said, thinking to himself that he would teach his feckless son a lesson, believing that before the next full moon appeared his son would abdicate the throne as easily as he had abdicated what little sense he had been born with.

But the good king had not anticipated, nor properly calculated the pernicious influence that Devadatta had over his son, for immediately the prince began to rule under the direction of Devadatta, he sent a party of men to take the Buddha's life.

King Ajatasattu assembled a new guard and put them under the command of Devadatta, who had devised a wily plan for the murder of the Buddha. He took one of the officers aside and gave him instructions, telling him which path he must return by once the deed was done. He next put two men on that path and told them to kill the man who came their way, and then to turn and come down another path, where he would post four men to kill those two, who would next be met on their designated path by eight men, who would next be murdered by sixteen officers. In this way, Devadatta believed it would be impossible to trace the Buddha's murderer.

The officer who was to kill the Buddha went forward armed with shield and sword. Knowing the Buddha's habits, Devadatta told the officer where he could be found. Creeping through the underbrush, the soldier spied the Buddha walking in widening circles around a large banyan tree, deep in thought. As the officer drew closer a sense of peace and well-being overcame him that was alarming in its unexpectedness, and yet so freeing that he felt nakedly revealed, not just to the Buddha but to himself. Inside his chest, he heard the words, "Come forward, do not be afraid."

He moved toward the disembodied sound to next hear the same words repeated, but this time in the human voice of the Buddha.

He stumbled forward, overwhelmed both by the light surrounding the Buddha and his own sense of shame. He fell to his knees and cried, "Forgive my transgression, Lord, I came here with evil intentions and I cannot believe now what it was I actually meant to do."

"Rise," Buddha said, "to see oneself as you have is in itself an atonement. You have moved from darkness into light, and having remembered yourself in this way, such experiences as this will repeat and grow in strength until you achieve consciousness. To take responsibility for your actions is to suffer yourself, and it is this suffering that enables one to grow. Some day you will be equal to the truth, for now it is enough that you see yourself as you are, without judgment or criticism in relation to this truth. Slowly, slowly, the gap between the two will close, and the day will come when you will know what it means to be One."

Calling him Friend, Buddha dismissed the soldier and put him on a path different from the one he had been instructed to take, and then he waited for the next two soldiers to arrive.

His plan foiled, Devadatta realized that the burden of killing the Buddha had now fallen to him. He climbed Vulture Peak Rock, this being one of Buddha's favorite haunts, and waited for Gautama to pass underneath. He made ready with a large boulder and at the moment when Gautama passed underneath he rolled the stone over the edge of the cliff. The Buddha heard the boulder come crashing down and jumped aside, but a splinter from the great stone gashed his foot, leaving a terrible wound.

The Buddha's foot healed slowly and caused him much suffering, but, while recovering, his thoughts were not on himself but on the state of those who believed that their fortunes could be improved through the misfortunes of others.

The monks had begun to assemble round the Buddha's dwelling place, chanting prayers and incantations for his recovery and lamenting the attempted murder.

Buddha called Ananda to his side. "What is all this clamoring about, Ananda?"

"They are standing guard, Lord, and chanting protective incantations."

"In that case, go tell them that the Perfect One's life cannot be taken by violence. This can never happen. Tell them to go about their lives; their presences are not needed here."

At that time, a wild, man-killing elephant by the name of Nalagiri was housed in the king's stables. Devadatta bribed the elephant keepers into letting the elephant loose on the road the Buddha traveled every morning with his monks, now that he was well enough to go into town for alms.

When the elephant appeared on the road, the Buddha did not waver, but his monks fled into the bushes at the side of the road and pleaded with him to follow. "It is Nalagiri, Lord! Please, Lord, run for your life."

Buddha was unperturbed and called to the monks to join him. "Do not be afraid, my life cannot be taken by violence. I did not achieve nirvana by means of violence, therefore violence cannot harm me."

The trembling monks did not move from behind the bushes, but watched as Nalagiri trumpeted and—with his ears forward and tail erect—began to charge the robed figure that seemed to be challenging him.

As Nalagiri entered the Buddha's vibrational field, he was suddenly encompassed by the Buddha's thoughts of loving kindness. He dug his hoofs into the ground, sending a spray of dust into the air. At once Nalagiri stopped directly in front of the Buddha, and with his tail and ears in repose and his trunk lowered to the ground, he bent his head before the Buddha, who patted him lovingly on his forehead.

Nalagiri drew the dust from Gautama's feet with his trunk and sprinkled it on his head, and with his eyes trained on the Buddha's forehead, he walked backwards, slowly, until he was out of sight.

The people who had supported Devadatta in his wickedness came to their senses when they saw that the forces of destruction unleashed by Devadatta had been transformed into forces for good, and now that their faith in goodness had been restored, the Sangha was again revered by them and held in high esteem.

The Buddha called for a gathering in the Service Hall so he could address his monks. "What is it we have learned from our ordeal with the wayward monk, Devadatta?" he asked the monks. "I will tell you a story. Once there was a small family of elderly elephants who lived near a large pond deep in the forest. They would wade into the pond and pull up lotus stalks with their trunks, and after washing them clean of mud they would eat them. These lotus stalks were good not only for their health but also for their looks.

"Now some young calves who had observed them from a distance thought that by imitating their actions they could receive the same results. But after pulling up the stalks, they began to chew them up without first cleaning them of mud. As a result, they became deathly ill and soon perished.

"This is how it must ever be for those who wish to be like others but who are not yet themselves."

twenty-four

I<small>T HAD BEEN</small> many years since Gautama had seen his friend, King Pasenadi, who was a long-time adherent of the Dhamma. Then one day, unannounced, King Pasenadi tapped on Gautama's door.

"Enter, enter!" Buddha exclaimed, upon seeing his friend, while observing at once that the king was in a troubled state. "How pleased I am to see you. Come now, sit down, and unburden yourself to your old friend. Tell me what brings you here?"

"I am free of my estate," the king began. "I am too old to rule, nor do I care to rule. All things end, and the ending of things is good, just as their beginning was good. Now I have time, as I never had before, to be in the moment, knowing how precious and fleeting is time.

"Today I was taken in my carriage to the pleasure park in Nagaraka, and wandering among the ancient, noble trees, I was reminded of the Perfect One, whom I often encountered in such settings in olden days. So I asked my attendants, 'Where is the Perfect One now, where does he reside?' and they said you were now in Medalumpa, just three leagues away, and so I made the coaches ready and that is how I have come to your door."

"Your wife, the queen, is not here," Buddha said. "Has she passed?"

The king hesitated and composed himself before speaking. "An irreconcilable loss," he answered, and holding his head in his hands, he repeated again and again, "irreconcilable, irreconcilable."

"I understand," Buddha said.

"After all this time, I cannot speak of it without breaking down."

"I understand," the Buddha repeated and looked at his friend with compassion. "We are now eighty, King Pasenadi. Did you remember that our ages are the same?"

"Ah, yes, Lord, I remember, of course. What can one say, youth vanishes, health vanishes, life vanishes."

Gautama considered how best to alleviate his friend's suffering, knowing he could only answer truthfully from his own experience of aging and the inexorable march of time across the landscape of human life. When he was ready to speak, he did so in verse.

> To be shamed by aging
> By the maker of ugliness,

To have one's grace trampled upon—
What is one to say?
Even to live to one hundred years
Is not to cheat that which gives no quarter.

King Pasenadi smiled in agreement with the Buddha's words. Seeing that his friend was in acceptance of his suffering, Gautama asked, "Great and honored king, if your chief aide who you trusted among all me were to come to you and say, 'Sire, there is a mountain as high as the heavens advancing from the East, and crushing everything in its wake.' And now came a man from the West with identical news, and likewise a man from the North and then another from the South, so that you knew all humanity would be destroyed. What would you do?"

"What I could do, Lord, at such times—and I have faced times that seemed as nearly hopeless as that—but to continue to walk in the Dhamma, to cultivate what is wholesome and make merit."

"So it has always been with me, and so it is now for us with old age and death closing in upon us. Nothing has changed, we go on as before, but with wisdom accumulated over a lifetime. Honored king, you understand the value of the Dhamma in ways now that would not have been possible before. I say again, The Dhamma is good in the beginning, good in the middle, good in the end."

One rainy season had passed and then another, when Gautama called to Ananda that they would journey next to Beluvagamaka. However, soon after they had settled into their quarters, Gautama took to his bed with an undiagnosed illness. Although he was in great pain he did not cry out, but retained his mindfulness with full attention on his weakened state until he was well again.

As soon as he was able, he rose from his bed and entered the Study Hall, sitting by himself at the back of the room. Ananda entered the hall with several other monks and took a seat across from the Buddha. "Lord, seeing you well again has restored my faith in your well-being. Since you became ill my own body has felt rigid, all my thoughts had blurred and my mind felt impaired. But I knew you would not leave us without first addressing the Sangha."

Gautama replied by challenging Ananda. "But what do you need that you haven't received? There is no secret version of the Dhamma. The only monks who would require a final pronouncement from me are those who think the Sangha depends on me, or else there is one here who thinks he should command the Sangha when I am gone. Certainly you know, being the person closest to me, that I have never believed that the Sangha depends on me or belongs to me in any way.

"I am now past eighty, Ananda, and my body, like an old cart, is starting to break down and is in want of repairs. But when I can sit and return to the heart abode, all else falls away, and I am at one with what is. In this way, each monk must become an island, with no other refuge, making the Dhamma their island as well, likewise, with no other refuge. These will become my children when I am gone, for they will have known for themselves why they have trained and what it is they serve."

At this time Gautama was living apart from his two chief disciples. While Gautama was residing in Jeta's Grove, Sariputta was living at the Sangha in Majaddan country. It was here that he fell into his final illness and after prolonged suffering passed on. His attendant, the novice Cunda, gathered Sariputta's bowl and robes and brought them to Ananda at Jeta's Grove. "Lord, I bring you these belongings of the venerable Sariputta, who has attained final nirvana."

Ananda was shaken by the news. He embraced Cunda, too overcome with sadness to speak. At last, collecting himself, he said, "Cunda, come with me; we must take Sariputta's bowl and robes to the Blessed One, and you can tell him yourself what you have told me."

After they paid homage to the Buddha, Cunda presented Sariputta's bowl and robes to the Buddha, explaining that his master had attained final nirvana.

With deep reverence, Gautama accepted his disciple's robes. He folded them neatly and placed them at his side, centering Sariputta's bowl face down on his robes. He looked from Cunda's downcast face to Ananda, who was weeping. "What is it?" Gautama asked Ananda.

"Lord, when I received the news of Sariputta's passing, I was so shaken I could not speak, and even now my thoughts are in such a whirl that I cannot even say what it is I am feeling."

"Brace yourself, Ananda. It is not as if the code that Sariputta followed all these years has been broken."

"It is not that, Lord, it is that he was our helpmate and guide, instructing and encouraging us, a tireless teacher of the Dhamma."

"Have I not told you countless times that there must one day come a parting from all that is beloved. Birth leads to dissolution. We are formed into being, we endure for a time, and then we fall. This is the law of nature. Everything that becomes must inevitably cease to be. Just as the strongest, most deeply rooted tree must one day fall, so too must man.

"Sariputta leaves behind a solid community that stands on firm ground and that will abide. Make of yourself an island; this is your only refuge in life. Make of the Dhamma your island; this is your only refuge in being."

Soon after Sariputta's passing, Moggallana also died. When the news reached the Sangha in Jeta's Grove, all the monks went out into the open to seek Buddha, who was sitting alone in mourning by his favorite banyan tree. After a long silence he looked up at the yellow-robed monks, and bathed himself in the serenity of their peaceful faces. Then he spoke: "From the beginning, for as far back as we can see, each Buddha has had two disciples like Sariputta and Moggallana. Thus it has been and so it will be in the future. It is a marvel beyond the telling, a wonder and a joy, that the Buddha had two such disciples who were loved and respected and revered by the Sangha, and whose example has been such an instrument of good. No more can I look out and know that Sariputta and Moggallana are somewhere doing their work. Even though they are missed I am not sorrowed by this, knowing that all who are born, formed into being, must pass away. Let all things be: sorrow, joy, triumph, defeat—and all else that comes to go. These are our experiences, but what we take from them is understanding, and this understanding is ours. This is what remains when we attain our final nirvana."

twenty-five

THEY HAD BEEN residing for some time in Vesal. One morning, Buddha announced his plan for the day. "Come, Ananda, take up our mats and let us go to Capala Shrine and pass the day."

When they arrived in the park, they placed their mats beneath the giant branches of one of the tree-shrines sacred to the Yakshas. "How pleasant is this park, Ananda. Here we can ruminate on our lives, and make our confessions to the gods if we like."

"It is as you say," Ananda answered.

"You know, don't you, Ananda, that the Buddha, being fully realized, can live out the remainder of this age, if he so wishes."

As he had done before, Buddha was laying out a hint for Ananda, or was it a trap, because unless Gautama was challenged he could relinquish his hold on life and attain final nirvana. Having accomplished his mission, perhaps the Buddha had grown tired of life. Was he feeling that it was time for him to complete his final round of earthly existences, that he was now to enter eternity, never to return again to this karmic realm of unending transmissions? Or was he begging to stay, and torn between his love of mankind and his yearning for release from the coil of life? Did he wish to hold on for another season—for another day such as today?

We do not know and Ananda did not guess what was on his mind, answering only in silence until the Buddha asked again.

Again, Ananda did not reply.

Had Mara, who was hovering overhead, captured Ananda's tongue or dulled his mind, so that he could neither think nor speak?

Again Buddha spoke and now for the third time Ananda did not answer.

"Leave me, Ananda," Buddha commanded, "Go do what you like."

Startled, Ananda rose to his feet and went and sat under a nearby tree where he would be hidden from the Buddha by the creepers cascading from the tree's branches.

Now Mara descended and addressed the Buddha. "It is time for the Blessed One's final nirvana," he declared, believing the Buddha had set his own trap and would not be able to extricate himself.

"All along you have believed yourself to be my equal," Buddha answered, "even though I have silenced you again and again."

Mara did not answer, believing, as he had so often, that this time he had the advantage.

"I will not leave," Buddha said now, "until the teaching has been accomplished."

"This has been done."

"The Dhamma perfected."

"Done."

"It's permanence established, its future longevity and influence assured."

"Done! Done! Done!" Mara fumed.

"Rest assured then, Mara, that I will now depart, my mission fully accomplished. In three months time I will be gone."

Mara realized in that moment that he had been truly vanquished, for the Buddha had accomplished his mission and was leaving of his own accord.

Buddha continued sitting, and concentrating his force, he intentionally loosened the will he held over his body, causing the formation of his material self to rumble out from his being until the entire region under his spiritual command began to quake, making a fearful sound that could be heard for hundreds of miles around.

When the ground had stopped shaking, Ananda got up from his seat and hurried to Buddha's side. "Lord, were those the drums of heaven just now, signaling the advance of the chariots of fire? I sense that something has been vanquished in order for something else to be received."

Buddha answered in verse:

"I have renounced my will over life
Loosening the spirit from its sheath
Like a warrior shedding his coat of mail."

"You were the cause then of the earth's rocking motion?" Ananda asked.

"There are eight occasions, Ananda, for the earth's quaking. I will name four: when a Bodhisattva travels from heaven and arrives in his mother's womb; when a Boddhisattva, mindful and fully aware, emerges from his mother's womb; when a Perfect One achieves full enlightenment; and when a Perfect One attains final nirvana."

Ananda began to tremble, for he understood now what the Buddha had been hinting at just before he was abruptly dismissed. He pleaded with his Master and life-long friend not to give up his life. "Please, Lord, live out the age for the good of heaven and earth, out of compassion for men and all living creatures."

"You know as I do, Ananda, that the Perfect One must ask three times before he can relinquish his life, and if unchallenged the decision is irreversible. Many times before I hinted at what was to come; that in time, for all of us, there is a separation and parting from our loved ones. Do you not remember all the warnings I gave in preparation for this moment—at Vulture Peak Rock, on the Robber's Cliff, at the slopes of the Vebhara, in the Sattapanni Cave, on the Black Rock overlooking Isigili, at the Overhanging Rock of the Serpent's Pool in the Cool Grove, then again at the Park of the Hot Spring, in the Bamboo Grove, the Squirrels' Sanctuary, at the Mango Grove and Deer Park?

"Now it is done. In three months time I will make my departure. Collect our things, and we will take ourselves to the Pointed Roof in the Great Wood."

Yasodhara now appeared before the Buddha in supernatural form. "Lord, allow me to enter nirvana now, in advance of your departure. My work is completed. I wish to join your mother in preparation of your arrival."

Buddha looked at his wife and gave his consent by raising his arms to the heavens. Standing before the light of the world, Yasodhara pleaded for forgiveness for any transgressions she may have committed. In the next instant she vanished within the same light in which she had appeared.

Gathering his retinue of monks, Gautama began traveling from Sangha to Sangha, attempting to reach as many of his monks and nuns as possible in his remaining time. He began by summarizing the basic tenets of the teaching. At the first gathering in Service Hall he exhorted the monks to be attentive to the four foundations of mindfulness, the four right endeavors, the four bases for success, the five spiritual faculties, the five spiritual powers, the seven enlightenment factors, and the Noble Eightfold Path.

"You do this for yourselves," he concluded, "you do it for your fellow man, and you do it for the gods." Then he said to them in free verse:

> Now I have made my refuge
> And it is time to depart.
> Study every action, every thought
> And most of all keep watch over your hearts.
> Devote yourselves to the Dhamma
> Until the painful round of rebirths cease.

Then, with Ananda at his side, he walked to a bluff overlooking the city of Vesali, and sitting with his back to the warming sun, he watched over the copper-roofed houses until the clouds on the horizon turned a brilliant orange and then into slivers of pink as the day passed slowly into the grey-dark dusk of night.

"Now I leave Vesali, Ananda, never to pass this way again."

twenty-six

VISITING THE SANGHAS along the Hiranyavati River in Malla Country, Gautama stopped for a two-week rest in Bhoganajara, where he addressed a large assembly of monks. "Now the time will come when you must reassess the teaching from the sources available to you, which will include your memory of my talks, or from a community of elders and leaders, or from some who are specialists in their memorization of the codes, or experts in the Traditions. Each may insist, and you may believe, that this is the Dhamma, this is the Discipline, this is the Master's teaching."

"When this time comes, it is imperative that you stand impartially before everything outside your own experience and verify for yourselves if what you have learned or been taught is confirmed by the Vinaya or in the Sutras. Only then can you judge if what you have heard comes from the Blessed One, for not all learning is correct, not all teaching is accurate, and you must refine your judgement and trust in your own integrity."

From Bhoganajara the Buddha traveled next to Pava, where they stopped to rest in a mango grove belonging to Cunda, the wealthy son of a goldsmith. When Cunda learned that the Buddha had stopped in his mango grove, after paying homage, he invited him to have his next meal at his home.

Arriving with his monks the next morning, Gautama took the seat prepared for him beside his host. "I have prepared a special dish of mushrooms and truffles for the Blessed One," Cunda said.

Buddha examined the dish before speaking. "I will have this; the monks may be served from the other dishes you have prepared."

After the meal had been taken, Buddha put his bowl aside, but before giving a Dhamma talk, he said to Cunda, "Bury this special dish you have made in a hole, for no one in this world can digest its contents, neither Brahmin, Maras, princes, or ordinary men."

Cunda whispered to Ananda that he feared his dish had made the Buddha ill, for it was evident by the way the Buddha was holding his side and from the sweat appearing on his brow that he had difficulty at times composing his words.

When Gautama had finished his talk, Ananda helped him to his feet and conveyed Cunda's concern for the Buddha's well-being. "He had wanted to make a special meal for you, Lord. The thought that he has made you ill has filled him with remorse and grief."

"Even should it hasten my death, he need feel no remorse. Tell him that even if this is to be the last meal before my death, it is valued as being equal to the dish of rice gruel prepared by the village girl, Sujata, just before my enlightenment."

When Ananda returned to the Buddha's side after consoling Cunda, the Buddha said, "Come now, we will go to Kusinara."

They had not gone far before Buddha stopped and asked Ananda to prepare a seat for him beneath a tree. "I am thirsty, Ananda, go fetch me some water from the stream we just crossed."

"Lord, the farmers in ox-carts that were on the road just behind us have churned up the water. It will not be fit to drink until the mud has settled."

"Go, Ananda, I need to drink now."

"But Lord, the water is undrinkable."

"Now, Ananda."

Ananda reluctantly rose to his feet and trudged to the stream. Kneeling on the bank above the mud-stirred water, he lowered the Buddha's bowl. To his amazement the water entering his bowl was clear and fresh and undisturbed.

The Buddha slept fitfully that night and in the morning they set out again for Kusinara, travelling in slow stages. When they reached Nairanja River, they were met by a commercial caravan led by a Mallian named Pukkusa who had once been a disciple of Ajara Kalama, but who, after leaving the order, had become a rich merchant. Gautama, remembering his youthful discipleship under Ajara Kalama, was pleasantly disposed to receive the Mallian merchant, who came forward to meet the Buddha bearing two shiny robes of gold cloth. "You will honor me by accepting these, Lord," Pukkusa begged, fearing his offering would be refused. Buddha acquiesced, understanding Pukkusa's need to make a connection once again with the path he had left so many years before.

When the merchant departed and they were alone again, Gautama watched as Ananda dressed himself, and then helped Gautama on with his golden robe. "How interesting," Gautama said. "As the giving of these robes put Pukkusa in touch with his own abandoned past, the donning of these robes reminds me of our origins as Sakyan nobles." Ananda nodded in agreement, but when he stepped back to admire the Buddha, he was amazed to see that the golden robe that had glowed in his hands just moments before had now lost all of its luster, for it was the Buddha that shone now, while the garment by comparison became a pale, lackluster yellow.

"This is a marvel, Lord. Can you feel what I see?"

"This is a transformation that can happen but twice in a Buddha's life, causing this sheen of bright, emanating gold to appear upon my countenance, making the skin clear and free of its aging components: Once, on the eve of his enlightenment, and then on the eve of his final nirvana. In the first instance it is the result of the abandonment of his former life, in the second instance it is the release of whatever clinging to life still remains.

"Now we will remove these robes and bathe in the river, and after I have taken my rest, we will go to the Sala Grove at Kusinara, named after the twin sala trees that grow there."

twenty-seven

SLEEPING WITH HIS head to the north between the twin sala trees, Gautama had laid down to rest in the lion's sleeping pose, with one foot resting upon the other, in a state of mindful awareness. While asleep, in full consciousness, he became aware that powder of sandalwood and petals of mandarava flowers were falling from the heavens. Those in attendance watched in veneration as the powder spread evenly over the Buddha's body, and as it fell, the singing of angelic voices could be heard above the clouds.

Gautama opened his eyes to the blossoming flowers of the twin sala trees, and all marveled, as this was not their season for flowering.

"The leaves honor you, Lord," those closest to him said, bowing in reverence.

"This is not the highest honor," Gautama said, turning to Ananda. "The highest honor for the Blessed One comes from the monks who walk in the Dhamma. Therefore, pledge yourselves anew once again before I depart, that you will walk in the Dhamma, that you will venerate and respect and honor the Dhamma."

All answered, "In this you have our pledge."

Ananda was too overwhelmed to answer with the others, and removed himself from the Buddha's sight. Leaning against a tree, he began to weep and commiserate with himself. "My Lord, who is about to attain final nirvana, is thinking only of my welfare, and after all this time I have not attained enlightenment."

Sensing Ananda's absence, the recumbent Buddha asked where he had gone.

"Lord, Ananda was overtaken by your compassion, and feeling remorse at his own inability to attain enlightenment, he has removed himself from your presence."

Knowing what was in Ananda's heart, the Buddha said, "Go to him and say, 'Your teacher wishes to see his friend.'"

Ananda composed himself and returned to his Master's side. "Do not lament my passing, Ananda. Have I not told you again and again that in this life we must face the departure of loved ones, for all that rises falls, and all that appears, disappears; but there is no death, there is only separation, and for this we must be prepared.

"No Buddha has ever had a more faithful attendant than you, who has served me with loving kindness and without reserve for all these years, and more than this you have instructed and guided

THE BUDDHA

those who walk the Dhamma. You have made great merit, Ananda, it will not be long before you attain Arahatship."

Gautama knew that all who heard the words addressed to Ananda would receive guidance for their own inner work, understanding that the greatest merit is earned by service, but that the privilege of service must first be earned.

Ananda was made free to let go and stand on his own, but the thought of his Master's departure was more than he could bear. "Lord," he pleaded, "do not attain final nirvana in this jungle village; let us go on to Benares, where you will be venerated by Brahmins, nobles, and warriors."

"It is beneath you to speak this way, Ananda. Go now into Kusinara and announce to the Mallians that this is the last watch, and that they should present themselves, that it not be said of them in the time to come that the Buddha died in their presence and they were not in attendance."

At Ananda's beckoning, the people came streaming out of the villages in great numbers, weeping and tearing at their hair, crying, "The final nirvana of the Buddha has come, soon the Eye of the Great One will vanish from the world."

Ananda was amazed at their grief, and understood as he had not quite understood before the powerful influence of his Master over the life of that place and indeed of the whole world as he knew it.

Ananda could see that he must not let each Mallian pass before the Buddha—for if he had, the night would pass and the lines would still be forming. He therefore quickly gathered the representatives from the various clans and instructed them to address the Buddha, naming their family, retinue, and friends, with the words, "We salute with honor the Blessed One, with our head at the Blessed One's feet."

Just as the organized procedure was about to begin, a wanderer by the name of Subhadda pushed his way through the crowd. "Perhaps it is more than mere chance," he thought, "that I find myself here in Kusinara at the last watch before the Buddha attains final nirvana. All these years I have wandered, wishing to believe, but unable to overcome my doubts. Now is my chance to challenge and be challenged, by putting myself before the Great One".

He approached Ananda. "Master, may I see the Buddha?'

When Ananda shook his head dismissively, Subhadda asked again. "I have been riddled by doubts all my life. I have never come this far before. How can I turn back, now that I have the Buddha in sight?"

"This is not the time. The Blessed One is tired; no one may approach."

Ananda refused Subhadda yet again, but with their voices raised their words reached the Buddha's ears, and he called out to Ananda. "Let him come; I know what he seeks. What I have to tell him he will quickly understand."

Subhadda paid homage to the Buddha and took his seat. "Lord, I would like to know, among all these monks and Brahmins, some of whom are even recognized as saints, if there are any who have achieved nirvana, and if one may receive direct transmission from them as they claim."

"Do not trouble yourself with this, Subhadda. I will teach you the Dhamma. Be still now and attend to my words."

As the Buddha spoke, the lamp of Dhamma was lit for Subhadda and his doubts erased. He knew now, with ultimate clarity, that he had spent his life avoiding the very thing he sought, and it was as if by magic that the Buddha had turned the coin and showed Subhadda what his life could be through belief, extinguishing what it had become through disbelief, freeing him to seek his higher self and become what he was born to be.

In the morning, Gautama called his monks to his side for the last time. "It may be that some of you still have doubts about the Dhamma, or concerns over the rules of the Sangha, or questions about your Path, or the way of transmission. Speak now, so that afterwards you will not say, 'I was face to face with my Teacher but could not speak.'"

Buddha waited for a response, but the monks—with heads bowed, many with tears in their eyes—could not speak.

"Do not be afraid. If you are in awe of me then tell your friend and let him ask for you."

With the silence still unbroken, Ananda said, "Lord, it is a wonder, it is a marvel, none speak because none have doubts about the Dhamma, the Sangha, or the Path that leads to enlightenment."

Buddha said, "You speak from the confidence of your faith, Ananda, but it is with direct knowledge that I can affirm your statement. Each of these monks has entered the Stream and is destined for enlightenment.

"Monks, all that appears must disappear, whatever rises dissolves. Work out your salvation with diligence."

Siddhartha the Gautama the Buddha, the Blessed One, having spoken his final words, in the heartbreak of silence left the world of appearances.

about the author

David Kherdian is the author of more than sixty books of fiction, poetry, nonfiction, and children's literature, including *Monkey: A Journey to the West* (Shambhala, 1992) He has won the Newbery Honor Book, Boston Globe/Horn Book Award, Lewis Carrol Bookshelf Award, Jane Addams Peace Award, and has been nominated for the National Book Award, and Friend of America Writers Award. He lives in Chatham, New York.

Wisdom Literature from White Cloud Press

Apprentice of the Heart
by Guy Finley
ISBN: 1-883991-58-7 / Paperback: $14.95

The Buddha Smiles: A Collection of Dharmatoons
by Mari Gayatri Stein
ISBN: 1-883991-28-5 / Paperback: $15.95

Creating Consciousness: A Study of Consciousness, Creativity, Evolution, and Violence by Albert Low
ISBN: 1-833991-39-0 / Paperback: $18.95

Waking Up In America by Ken Taub
ISBN: 1-883991-61-7 / Cloth: $16.95

Ways in Mystery by Luther Askeland
ISBN: 1-883991-16-1 / Paperback: $17.00

Wild Grace: Nature as a Spiritual Path by Eric Alan
ISBN: 1-883991-53-6 / Paperback: $24.95

Yin Yoga by Paul Grilley
ISBN: 1-833991-43-9 / Paperback: $15.95

For more information on these and other titles, visit:
www.whitecloudpress.com